DOORWAYS to Greater Faith

A personal and group study book

William D. Gainey

First Edition
All Rights Reserved
Copyright ©2009/2010

Copyright © 2009/2010 William D. Gainey
All rights reserved

First print by WestBow Press 12/21/2009
Printed in the United States of America,
Bloomington, Indiana.

ISBN: 978-1-4497-0006-5 (e)
ISBN: 978-1-4497-0007-2 (sc)
ISBN: 978-1-4497-0008-9 (hc)

Library of Congress Control Number: 2009942831

This book is printed on acid-free paper.

No portion of this book may be used without written permission and consent of the author. To contact the author, please refer to the information below with the "Author Contact Information" supplied for such permissions.

— Unless otherwise noted, all Bible quotations are taken from the New American Standard Bible®, © Copyright 1960, 1962, 1963, 1968, 1971, 1972, 1973, 1975, 1977, 1995 by The Lockman Foundation. Used by permission. (www.Lockman.org.)

— English Standard Version: Scripture quotations marked "ESV" are taken from The Holy Bible, English Standard Version. Copyright © 2000; 2001 by Crossway Bibles, a division of Good News Publishers. Used by permission. All rights reserved.

— King James Version (KJV): Public domain.

Author Contact Information:
William D. Gainey
2212 Red Fox Court
Murfreesboro TN 37129
(615) 890-6680

Publisher / Printer Information:
WestBow Press™
1663 Liberty Drive
Bloomington, IN 47403
www.westbowpress.com
Phone: 1-866-928-1240

Front Cover Design: Gina Lesnefsky

*"Yet He has now reconciled you in His fleshly body through death, in order to present you before Him holy and blameless and beyond reproach -- if indeed you continue in the **faith** firmly established and steadfast, and not moved away from the hope of the gospel that you have heard, which was proclaimed in all creation under heaven, and of which I, Paul, was made a minister... but has now been manifested to His saints, to whom God willed to make known what is the riches of the glory of this mystery among the Gentiles, which is Christ in you, the hope of glory."*
Colossians 1:22-23, 26b-27 (NASB)

*"For in it [the] righteousness of God is revealed from **faith** to **faith**; as it is written, "BUT THE RIGHTEOUS [man] SHALL LIVE BY FAITH."*
Romans 1:17 (NASB)

*"Nevertheless knowing that a man is not justified by the works of the Law but through **faith** in Christ Jesus, even we have believed in Christ Jesus, so that we may be justified by **faith** in Christ and not by the works of the Law; since by the works of the Law no flesh will be justified."*
Galatians 2:16 (NASB)

*"Now **faith** is the assurance of [things] hoped for, the conviction of things not seen."*
Hebrews 11:1 (NASB)

*"By **faith** we understand that the worlds were prepared by the word of God, so that what is seen was not made out of things which are visible."*
Hebrews 11:3 (NASB)

*"And without **faith** it is impossible to please [Him,] for he who comes to God must believe that He is and [that] He is a rewarder of those who seek Him."*
Hebrews 11:6 (NASB)

Blue Letter Bible: (NASB - New American Standard Bible).
Blue Letter Bible. 1996-2009. http://www.blueletterbible.org
Extraction date: 12 Oct 2009.

Appreciation and Dedication

First, I praise and thank God for His guidance upon my life and for the wonders of faith He showed me in the writing of this book. I dedicate this book to His glory.

I begin, also, by thanking my partner and my wife, Elizabeth (Liz), for her inspiration and encouragement through the years. She has continually stood by my side, helping greatly in the birthing process and production of this book. She is truly God sent to my life. Thank you, sweetheart!

We would also like to thank our daughter, Beth, and our son, Brad, for their help and encouragement in producing this book. Thanks also to Rita Lawrence for her help in proofreading, and to Gina Lesnefsky for the book cover. We thank our friends who have encouraged and prayed for the Lord's guidance for the writing of these pages. Finally, we thank our editor Debbie Christian, for her wisdom and encouragement. ☦

Table of Contents

Appreciation and Dedication 5

Prologue 8

The Definition of Faith 11

Part One

Faith Forming 17

Chapters
1: Faith Fixes Your Mind on Jesus 23
2: Faith Recognizes Authority 29
3: Faith Submits in Life's Trials 36
4: Faith Comes Boldly to Jesus 43
5: Faith Touches Jesus 49
6: Faith has No Brakes 55
7: Faith Presses On 62
8: Faith Remembers Jesus' Works 68
9: Faith is a Personal Relationship 75
10: Faith Moves Beyond the Ordinary 81

Part Two

Facets of Faith 91

Chapters
11: Examples of Faith at Work 95
12: God Honors Our Faith 102
13: The Risk Factor in Faith 109
14: Faith is Revolutionary 118
15: The Mind of Faith 125
16: Faith Moves Forward 133
17: Living by Faith—Part I 139
18: Living by Faith—Part II 146
19: Faith and Good People 153
20: Faith and Dreams 160
21: Faith and Mental Attitudes 171

Part Three

To Live by Faith 179

Chapters
22: Faith Knows to Do Right 185
23: Faith that Lives Forever 191
24: Faith that Requires Extraordinary Obedience . 198
25: Faith that Affects All Generations 205
26: Living by Faith 212
27: Called into a Life by Faith 219

Prologue

Faith is an overwhelming subject for many people, but especially for the Christian who struggles daily to find its meaning. We have such a desire for it, to know it and to walk steadfastly in the middle of it. For most of us, the truths of faith elude us as we grasp for it and for an understanding of it. The Lord is bringing His Church to a new thing, to an attitude toward faith that Jesus exhibited while on earth. This book examines the teachings of Jesus about faith, how it is formed and how it grows in the believer. Jesus came to reveal what you can do by faith.

At one point, the disciples asked Jesus to increase their faith. Jesus responded with an unexpected answer. He said, *"If you had faith like a mustard seed, you would say to this mulberry tree, 'Be uprooted and be planted in the sea;' and it would obey you"* (Luke 17:6). This is a great promise of the possibilities that were present for the disciples, and are present for us now in this great and not so mysterious area of faith.

PROLOGUE

We see in the Bible passages used in the upcoming part of this book that Jesus used the noun form of *faith*. Since Jesus spoke of *faith* in the noun form in His Faith-Forming School, we understand faith as a thing, a spiritual gift from God. Jesus was involved in teaching everything we need to know about salvation in the three years He spent in ministry. As we proceed here, we will delve into the things that Jesus taught about increasing faith. As you will see, each statement Jesus made about faith seems to be an orderly agenda on His part to show us how faith grows and is made well rounded and strong. Every time you hear someone speak of *well-rounded faith* think of the concept of *surround-sound stereo*, a sound that is full and true from every direction. This is how Jesus wants your faith to be. Jesus has us in His Faith-Forming School, and the diploma in His school is a degree in the obedience of faith. Romans 1:5.

In talking with Christians, a recurring request is that they want a greater understanding of faith. We know that the best times are ahead for the Church and for each believer who understands faith. What would happen if faith in Jesus Christ meant the same to us as it meant to the apostles and early believers? We can experience God and know that He guides our lives through His Spirit. Faith, being this wonderful gift of God, comes to us from heaven and opens us to the power of the Holy Spirit in Jesus Christ. It changes us in wonderful ways, healing individuals and families and relationships. It also reveals God in us to others who need Him. Faith is more than knowing facts about God. The Bible speaks of believers becoming so full of Jesus that they eagerly press on into a deeper relationship with God. Jesus becomes our reason for living, and God's love for us is more real. It is no wonder it pleases God and we gain His approval when we use His gift of faith. God said, *"The just shall live by his faith"* (Habakkuk 2:4 KJV). God gives us revelation about Himself in His word and about the importance of faith. *Faith is a great adventure even in this age; an age that thinks adventure in God is only a fantasy.* Faith is a true adventure for the Christian and it will grow more adventurous as the Christian grows closer to God. Faith is for here and now as much as it was for the renowned individuals God chose in the Bible. He has chosen you for this age, and the gift of faith He has for you is for right now. ✝

The Definition of Faith

Faith is so wonderful, like any gift out of heaven, that an attempt at a definition should begin with this truth: It is so fitted for human response that a little child can exercise it even without a definition. Yet, the very fact that faith does come to us from God hints that it may always move beyond our efforts to fully define it, and just like God, it will always remain wonderful. This keeps us forever grasping for the truths about it much the same as we continually grasp to understand our loving Father and His ways.

I like the tangle of words given in Hebrews 11:1 after the words: "*Now faith is...*" One gets the feeling he or she is about to receive God's definition of faith. "*Now faith is the assurance of things hoped for, the evidence of things not seen.*" But no, the tangle is too much, as if this wonder can't fit human words. I'm reminded of Paul's words in II Corinthians 12:2-4, when he was caught up into heaven. There, he saw things so wonderful that he spoke of hearing inexpressible words. He called them words man is not permitted to speak. In other words, human words cannot adequately describe certain spiritual things. Attempting a definition takes us on a trip through passages in the Bible and then it still falls short. Since *"wonderful"* also fits the attributes of our Godhead, one is faced with the truth that though gifts from heaven can be experienced and practiced in one's life, they cannot be fully described or defined using human words. This tangle of words in Hebrews 11:1 is therefore an attempt to form an image of the wonder of faith. Our inability to fully define it doesn't hinder or limit the work of faith in any way. By faith, we stand on the edge of Christ likeness. All we need to do is step out and start using our gift.

Let us examine the tangle that casts new understanding in our hearts and gives us a deeper look into faith. Again, Hebrews 11:1 says, *"Now faith is the assurance of things hoped for, the conviction of things not seen."* It sounds so simple, and it is absolute truth. It opens our eyes to know God. *"Faith is the assurance,"* the verse begins. As we continue on in the translation of our Scriptural text the word *assurance* in Greek means *"to stand under"* or *"to underlie the apparent."* Romans 1:20 says to us that God is *apparent*. His eternal power and divine nature have been clearly seen through what has been made, the creation. Faith is the foundation of the rest of the truth. Faith opens us to the spiritual truth that stands under the created physical realm and holds it together. Faith opens our understanding beyond physical truths, even on to God. However, this is not a definition. This is simply a description of still more of the wonder of faith. *Assurance* also can be translated as *substance*. Substance refers to tangible things, to that stuff from which things are

THE DEFINITION OF FAITH

made, like dirt or chemicals or other matter. Hebrews 11:3 says, *"By faith we understand that the worlds were prepared by the word of God, so that what is seen was not made out of things which are visible."*

Faith, then, is the assurance, or substance, of every truth of the Gospel; the cross, the resurrection of Jesus, eternal life, salvation, on and on we could go until all the gospel truths are listed. Faith believes all of this exists. Faith is the gift that gives us the assurance that rises up in us from God. It gives us the assurance that the gospel is true along with all the promises we hope for that God has given.

> *When we believe God's Words, we stand steadfastly in faith in all situations.*

It is interesting that the word, *hope,* in this same verse, means *confident expectation* in Greek. It does not mean *"maybe"* or *"perhaps"* or that one is *somewhat* convinced that a thing *might* happen. Faith opens the door that makes us confident that God is present to us. We still have not come to a concrete definition of faith. We simply see, by God's word what faith does, what it can do. By faith, we have sure evidence of God.

To illustrate its two-way access, here's how it worked in me in the first month of my experience with faith. After surrendering my life to God's will and determining I wanted to be like Jesus, I was so excited and sure, I was telling everybody about it. I started scouring the Bible. Before I got very far, I began to wonder, "Did anything really happen when I surrendered my life?" "Are my sins really forgiven?" The Accuser of the Brethren was busy. These questions haunted me and threatened the continued growth of my faith. I was in college at the time and hesitant to speak about it to the few Christians I knew. These questions were in my mind night and day. I would think of them all day and go to sleep at night asking the Lord about them. In the mornings I would roll out of bed to my knees asking God, "Did anything really happen when I gave my life to Jesus?" "Are my sins really forgiven?" One morning I awakened with these thoughts running through my mind: "Romans 5:1; Romans 8:1," over and over. That was interesting to me. I had no idea of what was in Romans. I had not finished reading the first four gospels, yet. I got to my feet and went to my classes all the while having "Romans 5:1, Romans 8:1" in the background of my mind all day long. About a week later, I suddenly had the greatest idea. I thought, "I'm going to look up those verses!" Many of us know these verses and they have become part of our ammunition against the wiles of our enemy. *"Therefore being justified by faith, we have peace with God through our Lord Jesus Christ"* (Romans 5:1 KJV). *"There is therefore now no condemnation to them which are in Christ Jesus, who walk not after the flesh, but after the Spirit"* (Romans 8:1 KJV). Double access! I talked to God and God talked to me. Once I had a hold of these verses, my whole demeanor changed. My insides felt as if they lighted and lightened up. That was faith. I knew God and God knew me and talked to me, cared for me, and worked a miracle in me. Faith gives everyone equal access to God, and faith is about a personal relationship with God that grows. In our daily lives, faith is the place of action where we allow the great adventure of God's leadership to happen. He protects us and guides us.

THE DEFINITION OF FAITH

Faith energizes so we grow beyond our own barriers that restrict us in life. It energizes us for growth beyond those things we use as excuses to return to our comfort and routines. Activated faith accepts God's invitation to live one's life for Jesus Christ, to be like Him. Faith is a way of life that undergirds and permeates everything we do. Faith is a deliberate and personal entrance into a relationship stirred by God who gifts us with faith.

As we proceed, we will see what Jesus has to teach us about growing faith. We may not be able to put a definition on it, but we can show evidence of it in our lives. Therefore, let us continue and see what Jesus has to teach us about greater faith. ✝

Part One

Jesus' Teachings on Faith

"Getting up, He went from there to the region of Judea and beyond the Jordan; crowds gathered around Him again, and, according to His custom, He once more began to teach them."
(Mark 10:1)

FAITH FORMING

When Jesus walked this earth as a man, He was on a mission that included faith forming. By faith forming, I am speaking of truths revealed by Jesus Christ that act to firm up, and strengthen and make our faith well-rounded until it is what Jesus called, *"Great Faith"* (Matthew 15:28). He is showing us everything we need to know about faith because the just shall live by faith. We shall live with the inner vitality that we see in Jesus. God was, and still is reaching out to mankind. He has also promised us that those of us who search for Him will find Him.

The Bible teaches that God is wonderful in counsel and magnificent in wisdom. He comes, saying, *"Come to Me, all who are weary and heavy-laden, and I will give you rest. Take My yoke upon you and learn from Me, for I am gentle and humble in heart, and you will find rest for your souls. For My yoke is easy and My burden is light"* (Matthew 11:28-30).

God is wonderful in counsel and magnificent in wisdom.

DOORWAYS to Greater Faith

What a gentle way for God to come to us, to all who want to know Him. We all need a gentle touch from God. We learn more eagerly and thoroughly from someone who loves us. We tend to resist someone who tries to browbeat us, and this is not God's method of teaching. As I sought to learn about faith from the Teacher, Jesus Christ, I saw a pattern emerging, and an expanding growth presented in His teachings on faith. In my studies, I came to Matthew 9:27, where two blind men came to Jesus for healing. We are often blind to the full wonder and even confused regarding faith in our lives. The two blind men came, crying out, *"Have mercy on us, Son of David."* Jesus asked if they believed He was able to have mercy and heal their sight. *"Yes, Lord,"* they answered. It seems many of us, too, are spiritually blind to the advantages that are ours, "by faith." Jesus touched their eyes saying, *"It shall be done to you according to your faith."* Most of us willingly admit we are not where we want to be in our faith as yet. The uncomfortable question for most of us arises: "According to *my* faith?" "Can't You do better than healing according to *my* faith, Lord?" Remember that one day Jesus wondered, *"... when the Son of Man comes, will He find faith on the earth?"* (Luke 18:8b) This hints of a time of weakened faith when we might make this kind of response:

> *Faith that is fully formed and understood frees one, for God works in you according to your faith.*

- **Blind Men**: Lord, did You say You would heal us according to our faith?
- **Jesus**: Yes.

PART ONE — FAITH FORMING

- **Blind Men**: Well, Lord, we've heard of Your mighty works. Ah, can't You do better than that?
- **Jesus**: Why yes, all authority in heaven and on earth is mine .
- **Blind Men**: Then why did You say it would be done according to *our* faith?
- **Jesus**: Because, child of God, I can give you only what you are open to receive. Even though all authority is Mine and I can do anything, I will not force Myself upon you. I have given you freedom. It would be unjust of Me to trespass upon your freedom to choose.

Faith is a gift of power that can permeate this earthly realm with the will and power of God that comes through the Holy Spirit. It is a gift that has to do with our openness to God. It is a gift that opens our heart, giving us access to God and giving God access to us. Just like children open their hands or hearts to receive a gift from their parents, we have to open our hearts to receive from God. God will not force us to open our hands and hearts to Him. Ephesians 2:8 reads: *"For by grace you have been saved through faith; and that not of yourselves, it is the gift of God."* Both grace and faith are gifts, but let us continue on with the topic of faith here. Faith is also given for our protection. I Peter 1:5 tells of those who are *"protected by the power of God through faith."* With regard to faith protecting us, it is also referred to as our shield (Ephesians 6:16) and a breastplate to protect us (I Thessalonians 5:8).

DOORWAYS to Greater Faith

God has given us a gift of faith through which a door of access, going both ways, opens between man and God. Through God's grace and justice, He has given man control of the door. You can open the door, hold out your hands, hold out your hearts, or not.

God's message to the Church, to the believers at Laodicea and to the believers today is this: *"Behold, I stand at the door and knock; if anyone hears My voice and opens the door, I will come in to him and will dine with him, and he with Me"* (Revelation 3:20). I am in charge at the door of my faith. You are in charge at the door of yours. Yes. *"It shall be done to you according to your faith."* See Matthew 9:29. Each of us is in charge of how far we are willing to go in our faith. God expresses this same truth with the word *"bind"*. *"I will give you the keys of the Kingdom of Heaven, and whatever you bind on earth shall have been bound in heaven, and whatever you loose on earth shall have been loosed in heaven"* (Matthew 16:19). Again, we have responsibility to act, according to this passage. "Whatever," includes the things one chooses by faith to believe or not believe; either is to be bound or loosed by our own actions. To bind a thing is to confine, prohibit or impede. To loosen a thing is to set it free. Faith that is not fully formed or understood actually can place limits on a person. Conversely, faith that is understood and utilized to its fullest will completely free us.

We are called to view every circumstance in our lives, good or bad, through our faith in Jesus Christ.

Since faith itself can free or impede us, the believer needs to nourish his faith. What God does for you indeed shall be done to you according to how you exercise your faith.

PART ONE — FAITH FORMING

Paul tells us, along with the prophet Habakkuk, that the righteous shall live by faith (Romans 1:17). Thereafter, from the moment we recognize our faith, our faith will be instrumental to how our door is positioned. We will be open to the wonders of our supernatural God or we, ourselves will be closed and the open doors of opportunity will be also. Our open doors will be limited if we remain undecided about what we will allow God to do in and through us.

Faith has the power to cause us to increasingly focus in our lives on Jesus Christ, giving Him access to granting all the vigor and vitality and hope He can give us. It is all in the name and power of Jesus. Our response and acknowledgment is what we contribute. The transformation in our lives is all up to Jesus! In this or any study of faith, we must focus first on Jesus, not on our faith. As in all subjects to do with this life in Christ, faith is another one that is founded on our Savior, and this is exactly how God intended our lives to be — in full surrender to the One and only living Son of God. In His teachings, Jesus reveals how to position our minds and attitudes so that He can form or grow faith in us.

Your faith is limited to what you decide you will allow God to do in you and through you.

The following chapters will trace the teachings of Jesus on faith forming in the men and women and even the children of faith. It is important to note that this study into faith is not a questioning of one's faith. The teachings of Jesus open us to the transformation and growth process in the faith we already have been offered by God. Let us receive it and go on to learn how to grow in it and become all that God has designed us to be in Christ. ☦

DOORWAYS to Greater Faith

Study Questions:

1. What benefits have you experienced by the truth that faith requires two-way communication between you and God?
2. What are some of the things that have limited your life of faith?
3. What activities and experiences have been most nourishing to your faith?
4. Are you willing, at this point, to open up your heart and mind to the gift of faith that God has for you? Do you realize now that it is something that is yours already?
5. Are you realizing in your spirit, at this time, that there is a deeper truth to the things of faith? Are you ready to explore them and move to a higher plane of glory in Christ?

CHAPTER 1

FAITH FIXES YOUR MIND ON JESUS
Matthew 6:25–33

The following ten chapters have to do with Jesus' building blocks of faith. As we have already established, Jesus speaks of faith many times in the four Gospels. A careful study of verses where Jesus speaks of the noun, *"faith,"* reveals a building pattern. We see a series of practices that reveal how He is able to reach increasingly deeper into our lives. As Jesus progresses in His teaching, He increasingly leads us into a deeper relationship with Him. Faith is and requires a conscious relationship with Jesus.

Jesus' first teaching has to do with the fixing of our minds on Him. That is basic and real for all of us. He is concerned that we experience progress in our faith. He immediately catches us up into His concern for our thought life, how we handle our anxieties.

DOORWAYS to Greater Faith

Our first experience with faith in Jesus is to rescue us from the thought life of the world. He tells us at the beginning of His ministry that the Spirit of God came upon Him, an anointing, so that He could proclaim release to captives, the recovery of sight to the blind (which includes the understanding of the truths of God's Word), and to free the oppressed (Luke 4:18). The purpose of faith in Christ is to affect a rescue in each of us from what we have let the attitudes of this world's culture do to us. We have each allowed our culture to hamper our faith.

Faith in Christ rescues us from the attitudes and platitudes of the world.

There is something in each person of faith from which we need to be set free. This world imprisons our minds and limits our ability to see truth. Faith brings us to Jesus for help and opens our eyes to God's wisdom. Faith gives us access to God's throne of grace and opens His access to our minds and hearts. Our task is to open the door to our hearts and minds, relax, and dine with Him as He works wholeness in us. He stands at the door of our hearts and knocks. We answered the door to receive Him and have fellowship. Now we are responsible to keep the door open for God to make us more like Christ. This mindset is opposite the world's attitudes that keep us in the enemy's grasp. We have newfound peace that sets us free. We rest in God and trust Him as we surrender ourselves for Him to mold us like no other potter can do! We just keep our eyes focused on the example He sent us, which is His Son, Jesus. Why worry! We've learned the uselessness of worry and anxiety, even though we still act as if worry will work something good the next time. So far, it has only served to pile up today's

1: FAITH FIXES YOUR MIND ON JESUS

worries on top of yesterday's. Jesus teaches that worry and anxiety focuses our lives toward the wrong direction. In contrast, faith aims us in the right direction. An example of this is seen in Romans 4:19-20 where Abraham is held up as an example of faith. He looked at his old body, about a hundred years old, and still believed God's promise that he and his ninety-year-old wife, Sarah, would have a baby. He cast aside the world's knowledge that would say, "Impossible," and grew stronger in faith by worshipping God and believing His promise. Faith is about believing and trusting in Jesus. Where we put our faith is the problem. Jesus is our way, and our truth, our very life. We are to allow Him to give us His eyes and understanding about these things. We are to focus on the growth into wholeness that is ours through faith in Jesus—growth from just physical world beings (our flesh bodies) into new beings in Christ (our spiritual bodies).

No matter how far along in faith we grow, we still struggle occasionally. We know these things, yet we still grow anxious about the physical life situations in which we live. We need to remember that Jesus lived in them too. He lived each day of His life, joyfully and wholly and adventurously. He lived in that joy while He was fully aware that His future on earth was to suffer for each of our sins on the cross. When His time came to fulfill the will of God, through His tears that flowed like blood, He prayed, "Not My will, Father, but Thy will be done." In this same way, we are to have the mind of Christ and surrender our lives to God and His will. The day is coming when the heart and de-

> *Faith is designed by God to lead us beyond worry to Jesus.*

sires of Christ expressed in His prayer above are going to be expressed in you and in me. We can have faith in our Savior as our example of living this life on earth. He loved and wept with His friends when they suffered loss. He cared for those who were sick. He spent His life in service to others and to God.

Each of us gets mired down with the tension of providing for our present lives. We experience captivity, a prison life and its oppression in such needs at times. The correct response to this tension is to let it bring us to Jesus in faith. We should cast our cares upon Him because He truly does care for us. Yet, we often lose our peace and wander elsewhere, looking for solutions in places we should never visit. I have discovered the reason God wants us to have peace and blesses us with peace so often is because we hear Him more clearly when we are at peace. We are more receptive to hearing His voice and the wisdom He has for us for our particular situation. I often hear God when I'm in the shower because the warm water washing over me soothes and relaxes me, and I experience a great sense of peace. For many of us, we enjoy time with the Lord early in the day before the business of our daily activities. Again, we are at peace, and these are the times when we can hear our Lord speaking clearly. Find those times for yourself because they are priceless. Jesus urges us not to worry, asking what will we eat, or drink, or wear, or do, or say, and all the other rag-tags of little faith. Worry and anxiety assume the created order has more truth in it than the Creator's order. It does not!

> *Worry and anxiety assume the created order has more truth in it than the Creator's order.*

1: FAITH FIXES YOUR MIND ON JESUS

Faith in Jesus calls us to a shift of our dependency as He calls us into a new life. Jesus reminds us that if God clothes the fields with grass, will He not much more clothe you? You of little faith! Read Matthew 6:30. Some translations make these two sentences into one. I like the way the translators in the New American Standard Bible separate this into two sentences. It doesn't include, "You of little faith," in the question. It is true that our faith is little when we are anxious. It is also a fact, as we will see later, that little faith can be as mighty as great faith. That is a supernatural marvel in itself. Notice this, that Jesus wants the best for us, not just the good. He wants us to have great faith. God does understand our weaknesses and He has promised to be our strength.

Right now, Jesus is in the first steps of teaching us about growing faith, of us discovering the wonder of who has gotten a hold on us through faith in Himself. He has a purpose in grasping hold of us! After years of growth and maturing, Paul speaks of pressing on, *"so that I may lay hold of that for which also I was laid hold of by Christ Jesus"* (Philippians 3:12). Of course, Jesus' purpose includes all the wonder of salvation now and in eternity. Right now we are thinking of the wonder of fixing our focus on Jesus Christ in the here and now, of learning more about faith and how Jesus wishes to form it in us. Here we learn to let

The circumstances of our lives are designed by God to increase our faith in Jesus.

Him remind us again and again and again, if necessary (and it is in my life), to return our thoughts to Him as we progress moment by moment through our day. Life is about Jesus. We are being taught here in Jesus' Faith-Forming School that we

DOORWAYS to Greater Faith

are to first take hold of Jesus in our thoughts. We are not to let the world or Satan deceive us by leading us into worry and anxiety. Fixing your mind on Jesus is step one in faith forming. How interesting. We are not to fix our eyes on our faith itself, as we all do intermittently in our attempts to grow our faith. We fall into self-deception when we think we can strengthen or grow our own faith. If we fall into this trap, we have turned our eyes away from Jesus again to ourselves. We become self-centered. Jesus alone is the giver and builder of our faith. Let us not be distracted from Him, ever. ☦

Study Questions:

1. What does "fixing your mind on Jesus," mean to you?
2. What do you need to be released or set free from in your own life?
3. How much has worry helped you?
4. What places or situations do you make for yourself or find yourself in where the peace of God allows you to hear from Him?
5. What are some ways to fix your mind on Jesus? What things transfer your mind and heart from a spirit of fear to a spirit of faith?

CHAPTER 2

FAITH RECOGNIZES AUTHORITY
Matthew 8:5-13

Jesus has more respect and confidence in us than we do in ourselves. We seem to think it takes years to be trained enough in faith for us to be any good at living for the Lord. Many who have believed for years think they are not ready to serve Him. As they practiced their faith using these teachings that we are considering, Jesus trained His disciples for three years, then released them into faithful service with an authority from the Spirit that turned the world right side up. Of course, the world thought this truth was upside down. In Acts 17:6, we read that a mob in Thessalonica, reacted to Paul's teaching, and at the prompting of some unbelieving Jews, grabbed Jason while shouting, *"These men who have upset the world (turned it upside down) have come here also."* When the world is faced with those who step outside and into a life with

DOORWAYS to Greater Faith

Christ, they feel that their world is turned upside down, when in fact, to follow Jesus, we become turned right side up.

Jesus' regard for us and His knowledge of us are so great, He knows we can enter into the use of our faith as soon as we hear and accept His teachings. He knows we were created and, in Him, empowered to be God's children. As we walk out what Jesus says about faith, living by faith becomes a part of our life, and we can begin to minister immediately by telling what Jesus has done in us. It is powerful in the lives of others when they not only hear this testimony, but they see the transformation in us. This is how it happened in me. It was powerful and quick. Our growth begins immediately. We often suffer at the hands of those who don't understand this change.

We are to expect Jesus to be extravagant in the faith-teaching circumstances that He puts in our lives.

Why does the Christian have to suffer? Why did Jesus have to suffer? We suffer because, as Jesus learned obedience through His suffering, we also grow in faith as we learn obedience through our own suffering. See Hebrews 5:8. Suffering is usually the best way we learn obedience. Just like our own children when they are punished for disobedience, they learn as they grow. We discipline them because we love them. If we don't discipline them, they grow up to be people not fit for society, but will always feel slighted because things don't go their way. They never learned the lessons we, as parents, are obligated by God to teach our children.

Suffering is a free college of sorts for the most valuable training in the world. Again, look at the degree we receive! It

2: FAITH RECOGNIZES AUTHORITY

is the degree of the obedience of faith (Romans 1:5). Obedience is one important characteristic worked in us by faith. It is not worked out by our power or ability. In our suffering, we learn that so much is beyond our control. We learn to look to Jesus and His authority over our lives.

This teaching on the relationship of faith and authority is found in Matthew 8:5-13. A centurion, a Roman, came asking Jesus to heal his young servant, a young boy. He was paralyzed, suffering intense pain. Having had a paralyzed sister-in-law for years, let me tell you that a paralyzed person does suffer pain. The physician, Luke, also tells us this young boy was near death (Luke 7:2).

When Jesus started to go to the centurion's home the centurion stopped Him. He felt unworthy to have Jesus enter his home. Notice that he called Jesus, "Lord." He knew who Jesus was and knew what Jesus could do. He told Jesus that he understood the concept of authority. He said he himself used authority in his line of work. "Just say the word, Jesus. I understand authority." This was how well the Roman centurion understood about the total power in the authoritative spoken word.

Understanding God's authority is another aspect of our growth in faith. What is so completely thrilling and revealing is how well the little children even understand it. They understand authority better than adults. I received an email about some praying children in a Church in Kenya. There are about 200 of them, ages three to seventeen. The country is very troubled and is full of fighting: President Mwai Kibaki fights against the opposition leader Raila. In the middle of the fighting the children pray. They pray for their country. Since they started praying, there have been no deaths in their slum area, no houses burned, not even any violence in their section of their slums. Adults have been amazed. The children, though, don't even mention it. They just go about playing and expect it to happen. They left it with God. How much do we expect to happen when we pray? The condition of our faith is exposed in our ability to expect. That is also where our understanding of authority is exposed. Let's pray with expectancy.

The condition of our faith is exposed in our ability to expect.

Let's look at the picture of these little praying children. One part of the email I read mentioned them leaving the prayer meeting. It was raining outside. They ran out into the rain laughing. Not one of those little children complained about the rain for it was raining a month early in the dry season. The rain was another answer to their heartfelt prayers. Yes, you can see how these children understand authority. You see, faith moves beyond our intellect. It really is *"the assurance (the substance, the evidence) of things hoped for."* See Hebrews 11:1.

Authority is the ability to produce an effect, or to influence it. The word for authority used here, *exousia*, is an authority that denies the presence of any hindrance. Faith is, then, the understanding of the absolute authority of Almighty God. Jesus marveled at the centurion's faith and understanding of the spoken Word of Jesus. Jesus had not found such great faith with anyone in Israel. Jesus marveled only two times in the Bible. The other time was in Mark 6:6 when He experienced the unbelief of the people in Nazareth.

2: FAITH RECOGNIZES AUTHORITY

They were astonished at Jesus' teaching, wisdom and miracles. Yet, they still had no faith. Jesus marveled at this lack of faith as much as he marveled over the centurion's complete faith. It is important that we understand the authority of Jesus for Him to grow our faith or for Him to do His work through us. Authority comes from God, and we understand that now. He gives it to His children, to any of us. Therefore the best way — the only way — to grow in your knowledge of authority is to grow in your personal relationship with Jesus who gives it. Everything God says in His Word is meant to enhance your faith in Jesus, which He gives you. God is not concerned about getting you to watch yourself or your growth or to act in any particular way. That is not the end of the matter as we sometimes hear. We are actually to lift our eyes up and away from the world's ways to see the ways of Jesus Christ. He died to redeem the world and make it perfectly whole and restored before the Father. Through Jesus, God was restoring His broken creation. The fact that in the process we can be saved by faith in Christ illustrates the authority that is in Jesus.

There is nothing easier than obtaining salvation. Take the gift of faith God gave you. Have an open heart and mind. Access Jesus and let Jesus access you. Open the door and you will find that it is already done. Hebrews 12:2 speaks of us fixing our eyes upon Jesus, Who is the One Who authored and finished, or perfected, this faith we are talking about. This means more than glancing at Him occasionally on a Sunday. The grammar of this verse speaks of a continuous viewing of Jesus — it means we

Jesus is approachable, and is pleased when you come to Him in your need.

seek an ongoing relationship with Jesus, giving Him our undivided attention. It is looking away from every other object and fixedly, earnestly looking to Jesus so as to see Him distinctly. Faith is the fixing of Jesus in your attention; so fixing Him that you increasingly become willingly engaged in the wonder of His authority, and His willingness for you to use it in obeying His will.

Let us be clear about the authority He imparts to us. It is for obedient service, not for positioning us to be recognized. Jesus is the One to be recognized and honored. As we fix our eyes on Jesus, we discover what He means for us to be doing.

You find the answers to what God wants you to be doing by reading His commands in the Bible and by listening to the commands He speaks to you right now. Recall how Peter waited for Jesus' command for him to walk on water. Remember Peter praying and waiting for Jesus' command concerning what he should do about Tabitha's death. Acts 9:40 says Peter knelt down and prayed, waiting for God to tell him what to do. After praying to God for direction and hearing God's answer, Peter stopped praying. Then, he turned to Tabitha's body and commanded, "Tabitha, arise." She did. Peter understood Jesus' authority working in him. He also understood that Jesus had given Peter His own authority to be used when and how Jesus directed him. Faith is about fixing our minds or hearts on Jesus and understanding the scope of His authority. God is here with us, directing us. We need to hear Him. He is heard in gentle thoughts and sometimes in difficult arguments going on in our minds that we can miss if we aren't attentive.

2: FAITH RECOGNIZES AUTHORITY

Step number two in the process of Jesus forming our faith is to understand Jesus' authority and how that works His will in us as we yield to His authority. ☨

Study Questions:

1. How assured are you concerning Jesus' high regard for you?
2. When would you like to begin exercising the faith that you have in the authority of Jesus Christ in you? Are you aware that it can begin today?
3. How do you think the centurion, who felt unworthy of Jesus' visit, could fully expect Jesus to heal his paralyzed servant?
4. What do you believe Jesus' authority will do in your life?
5. What plans do you think God has for you in relation to how Jesus works His authority through you? What changes could this authority make for your own life, your family, your neighborhood, your workplace, your town...?

CHAPTER 3

FAITH SUBMITS IN LIFE'S TRIALS
Matthew 8:18–27

The third step we'll talk about in rounding out our faith is allowing Jesus to be in charge of our lives. This is simply submitting our lives to Jesus. As these teachings of Jesus are understood and practiced in our lives, they will have a surround-sound, stereo effect. They will round out and firm up our faith.

Going back to chapter one, you will recall how the first step Jesus mentioned was the fixing of our mind on Him. The second step, in chapter two, is that we become increasingly aware of Jesus' authority in our lives, an authority that moves us beyond simple awareness into obedience toward His authority. The purpose of this book is to open us to the fullness of Jesus' plan for faith in our lives. Because Jesus has all authority, faith involves the ordering of our lives according to His words and promises. The third step is placing one's daily activity under

3: FAITH SUBMITS IN LIFE'S TRIALS

the control of Jesus, actually surrendering our daily activities to His guidance and God's will. In our Bible reading, a scribe came to Jesus and said, *"Teacher, I will follow You wherever You go."* Jesus' response indicates how He knew the scribe's heart. He was more interested in popularity than submission. Jesus' answer points to His own lowly circumstances, even though he was so popular that crowds of over 5000 people came in search of Him. He answered the scribe, *"The foxes have holes and the birds of the air have nests, but the Son of Man has nowhere to lay His head."* Jesus had no place on this earth to call His own.

As we serve Jesus, we are to strive to be like Him, and Jesus did not serve Himself. He served God and God's will. We are to have that kind of faith, those priorities in life and that kind of surrender. Another disciple asked Jesus for permission to go home and wait for his aging father to die before he followed the call Jesus had for his life. He seemed to think he could pick up or lay down his commitment and faith in Jesus at any time. He put his own concerns ahead of Jesus. However, when we surrender to His will, the surrender is to be with our whole heart. Actually, faith is a process of making Jesus our highest priority. In the Bible, it is plain to see that placing Jesus first actually can be done. God did not mean for us to have to struggle with faith, though most of us do. God gave us His Holy Spirit in order to give us the power we need to express and be obedient in our faith. Furthermore, the Spirit is God's assurance to us that His promises concerning faith are for you and for me.

Let us watch now as Jesus allows us to see His care for us. Mark 4:36 says that Jesus got His disciples into the boat to go to the other side of the Sea of Galilee. Note that Jesus was in charge, their obvious Leader. He put the disciples on that boat knowing the situation they faced on the sea. Someone once said the safest place a person can be is standing in the middle of a six-lane expressway during the rush hour, if that is where Jesus calls one to stand. Remember in Acts 8:26, how the Lord told Philip to leave a revival and go to a desert road leading from Jerusalem to Gaza? Philip went without any questions, to that hot, dry place, and led an Ethiopian eunuch to Christ, thus spreading the Gospel to Ethiopia. In the lesson about the boat, Jesus knew He put the disciples in the way of a storm. He was forming and strengthening their faith, giving them the next step of growth so the history recorded in the Book of Acts would be there, as another example, to show us how Jesus builds our faith. He had you in mind.

The great storm arose. Literally, the correct translation is "a great earthquake" or "a great turbulence" on the sea arose. Jesus has them there for a purpose. Then, Mark 4:38 tells us that Jesus went to the back of the boat and fell asleep on a cushion. Imagine the absurdity. Why did Jesus do this? Surely, it was more than just Jesus being exhausted and needing sleep. The disciples were tired, too. The great storm struck and the waves were lapping over the sides of the boat. Jesus began exhibiting His own faith. He knew the Father was keeping Him safe. There was no need for Him to worry. Faith is designed to lead us beyond worry to keep our focus on Jesus and to remember our God protects. The disciples still had this to learn. They looked at Jesus sleeping and felt like He didn't care. Have you ever had this similar feeling? There have been times when some have wondered where Jesus was and if He really cared.

3: FAITH SUBMITS IN LIFE'S TRIALS

The disciples had to wake Jesus! Where was their faith? It had washed overboard on one of those waves and fear replaced their faith. Matthew said they woke Jesus saying, "*Save us, Lord, we are perishing!*" Mark's report of this same incident reads, "*Teacher, do you not care that we are perishing?*" Here is the irony of this situation. They were in that storm because they obeyed, not because they disobeyed. They were in the storm because they *were* submitting to Jesus. Jesus slept because He was confident in God's will.

> *Do not allow discouragement to enter in when you ask God for help.*

He also slept to lead *them* into their next faith-forming step. Would they trust Jesus when He seemed to slight them? Would they have faith above the circumstances?

They did fail the test in trusting God and His will. Jesus also got them into the boat to assure them that they were where they were meant to be. Conversely, they did not fail the test of calling upon Jesus when they needed Him. They also discovered He came to their aid when they called. Jesus asked them a question that turned their attention to what was really occurring at school that day. "*Why are you afraid, you men of little faith?*" The whole exercise had been for them to see where their faith was and where it needed to be. This is no easy lesson. Circumstances seem more real than the invisible faith we need and have been given. They looked at their situation instead of finding faith within. Surely, each one of our situations has the same purpose — to see if we trust where Jesus has us and to see if we are submitted to God's purpose in our lives while there. Do we have faith in God or our situation?

DOORWAYS to Greater Faith

We, the Church, on Sunday—when everything is going our way—express our faith and openly worship God. Then, when trials arise, our eyes immediately stray from Jesus to the trial. We wonder, as we take our eyes off Jesus, where He is, while our eyes are so focused on the trial we become overwhelmed. The trial becomes so big because it is all we focus upon! Well, Jesus is right here with us where He has always been. He is bigger than the trial, if we would only focus and put our eyes where they should be. Our question, rather than, "Where is Jesus," should be, "Where is my faith?" We need to replace fear with faith in God.

> *In the face of potential death, both physical and spiritual, faith offers life, vitality and freedom.*

Christ could prevent the storms in our lives. If He did this, our faith would never grow. God doesn't settle for what is only good for our lives. He desires the best. Romans 5:3-5 tells us that tribulation in our lives brings about perseverance. Perseverance produces proven character. Proven character brings about hope. These events in our lives, rather than disappointing us, bring affirmation in our souls and spirits concerning God's love for us through the Holy Spirit. God has wonderful plans for our welfare and future in mind (Jeremiah 29:11).

The disciples' experience in that terrifying storm brought them to amazement and further revelation of the might and power of Jesus. They asked, "What kind of man is this, that even the winds and the seas obey Him?"

We've got to get a good understanding of the difference between faith and fear. In all of the events of our lives, we are experiencing God's very best for our faith to be strengthened.

3: FAITH SUBMITS IN LIFE'S TRIALS

As we go through these trials, we are in our School of Faith-Forming with the Lord. He is still the same with us as He was with the first disciples — training us, growing us. However, there is one difference, which is to our advantage. We have the Holy Spirit to guide and empower us.

God is completely trustworthy as He guides us through our life experiences. It is safe for us to be completely submissive to Him. Wherever we are, whatever is happening, He cares more for us than we do for ourselves. We would not face these trials if the choice was ours. We would be deformed Christians; refusing to face what God knows would make us more like Jesus. God has chosen the best experiences for us to impart the lessons of faith that He has planned for our lives. We would change many things, if we could! You know you would. I would! Wherever He calls us to be, He is there guarding us. He guards us even from our own selfishness and shortsightedness. All of life's trials we endure are for our benefit and growth. "One of your men puts to flight a thousand, for the Lord your God is He who fights for you, just as He promised you" (Joshua 23:10). Let us practice submission and total surrender to God's will on a moment-by-moment basis. ✝

Study Questions:

1. What are your priorities in life? Do you live for God, your family or yourself?
2. Are there times when you feel Jesus doesn't care? What do you believe you should do about those thoughts?

DOORWAYS to Greater Faith

3. What trials are you enduring? Do you see what God may be working out in it all?
4. In what ways can you be more submissive and attentive to Jesus in your trials?

CHAPTER 4

FAITH COMES BOLDLY TO JESUS
Matthew 9:2–8

Each facet in faith forming points us directly to Jesus. Jesus is the way and the truth and the life (See John 14:6). He holds our lives in His hands, as well as being our way to life through faith. He is the one who teaches us how faith works. Each facet in this series of teachings also strengthens or firms up our own personal faith.

This story of the paralytic and his four friends as reported in three of the Gospels — Matthew 9:2-13, Mark 2:3-12 and Luke 5:18-26 — is where we see the event begin with a crowd surrounding Jesus. The friends of the paralytic could not reach Jesus through the crowd for their friend. Therefore, they tore an opening through the roof and lowered the paralytic before Jesus, and watched. Jesus did not get flustered because of the interruption. There are other instances in the Bible where needy persons of faith interrupted Jesus. The woman who reached and touched the fringe of Jesus' robe; the children interrupting and sitting on His lap, Jesus had many interruptions. He just blessed those who interrupted Him. It makes you want to interrupt Him, doesn't it? He always responds favorably. Jesus is never too busy for your smallest or largest request!

Jesus saw their faith. Faith makes a way for us to approach Jesus. It does something; faith gives birth to action. Jesus' first words, after seeing their extraordinary faith were directed to the paralytic: *"Take courage, son; your sins are forgiven."* When Jesus said, *"take courage,"* it was a continuous command. The paralytic needed courage. We also need courage, and we need it continuously as we, too, take up a life of faith. Faith is foreign to those of us who have been caught up in the world's ways. Faith is a command into continuous boldness of mind with Jesus, continuous joy, continuous ability to approach Him and the Throne of God's grace. One might think, *but that's not my character.* After understanding faith, the ways of God *are* your ways. God has given you the right to become His child (John 1:12).

You have been made into a *new* creature that has become *new* because of your *faith* in Jesus. Ephesians 5:1 tells us to be imitators of Christ, or to strive to resemble Christ. Incidentally the word, "new," in II Corinthians 5:17, means "new in species," and "new in character," "unheard of," and "unusual," "something never even thought of," and therefore, "unimaginable" — a new creature. I'd be willing to be lowered through a roof to receive that, but we don't have to go to those extremes.

4: FAITH COMES BOLDLY TO JESUS

Those of faith are commanded to move into their new character quickly. Our transformation is immediate. The Bible tells us, "*Behold, now is the acceptable time, behold, now is the day of salvation*" (II Corinthians 6:2). Peter was struck in the side by an angel and told to get up, quickly (Acts 12:7). The sooner we move into what God is presently giving us, the less likely we are to yield to the human habit of backing away from the will of God. We back away from going forward into God's wonders and the new life He has for us, completely unaware that our enemy is trying to prevent us from entering into God's ways. As we look at the paralytic, we see how quickly Jesus moves. Jesus' response to the faith of the paralytic's friends, as mentioned above, was to forgive the paralytic's sins. We usually think the four friends got together to bring their friend to Jesus. The way Jesus immediately addressed the paralytic with forgiveness, it sounds like the paralytic talked his friends into bringing him!

Jesus tells us that the new life He gave us when we first expressed faith is so new and so full of vitality that we need new wineskins. Old wineskins, our old ways of life and even our old religious traditions, do not work anymore. New wineskins are made from sheep stomachs. It takes the death of a sheep to make a new wineskin. How appropriate is this example!? This means that in order to experience life, it requires the death of our old life. This is the cross we bear. When Jesus tells us to take up our cross, He means for us to lay down our old life and our old ways. We are ready for our new wineskins and our new life, aren't we? We have been experiencing spiritual paralysis. Because of the fallout left behind from sin in our lives, some believers have not entered into the fullness of what Jesus means for faith to work in us. Jesus immediately forgave the paralytic's sin. It was unexpected, because the paralytic came to be healed of his paralysis, not to have his sins forgiven. Jesus was loading His big guns, so to speak, to blow away doubt. Jesus tells the man that his sins are forgiven because the act of forgiving is not a visible action. Healing a man's paralysis is visible.

Here, then, is a different slant on authority. It is the authority Jesus has on earth to forgive sin, to do spiritual things within us, as well as to do physical things in our lives. Jesus' authority is such that absolutely nothing can hinder it. Nothing. The crowds were awestruck and glorified God who had given such authority to men, specifically to Jesus in this incident. Remember Jesus is fully God and fully man, both at the same time. Philippians 2:7 says Jesus emptied Himself of His deity. We celebrate this at Christmas. He emptied Himself when He became a man. Taking the form of a bondservant, He was made in the likeness of men. He was still God, but at the same time He was fully human, except He was without sin. See Hebrews 4:15. That Jesus emptied Himself means He willingly gave up His privileges as God, and walked this earth for more than thirty years as a man, doing all of His marvelous works and miracles, submitting Himself to the Father, praying for guidance in all situations, and obeying the Father. Therefore, Jesus demonstrated, for our benefit, the relationship between God and Adam before the Fall. These were perfectly beautiful days when God walked with Adam and Eve in the Garden. Imagine this. We have the same opportunity to walk

4: FAITH COMES BOLDLY TO JESUS

with God and approach Jesus with everything. We are called to follow Jesus, walk in His footsteps, and be like Him. That is also the reason I Corinthians 15:45 calls Jesus the second or last Adam. Those of faith are called to be the same as Adam was before the Fall. We are to be like Jesus, who demonstrated for us what Adam was like. Jesus came to show us the kind of life we are to live by faith. All of the activities Jesus did as a man, we are to be able to do. Jesus even tells us that because of the Holy Spirit, whom He sent, we will do even more! This opens the door of our mind to the reality of what faith is for us. Jesus provided the Way for it to be available. We just have to accept it, understand it and use it.

Jesus is the second Adam, living the life Adam was created to live, the life we are called to live now, by faith in Jesus.

In the Bible passage regarding the paralytic, his friends brought him to Jesus. Note Jesus' eagerness to commend and encourage and to forgive sin on the spot when, by faith, men interrupted Him. He is always ready to bless us. We see demonstrated here both the persistence of the friends and the paralytic. They did not hesitate at any obstacle and found a creative way to get to Jesus. The crowd did not and could not block them away; neither did a door that had them shut away from Jesus as the crowd pressed against it. A person of faith finds a way to get to Jesus. These things are good to know when the enemy mires us down in old patterns of timidity, depression, fear, or anything else he can use from our past. He will always work to keep us from approaching Jesus. Friends, we need to leave these parts of our old nature behind. The enemy has no power over you any longer as you begin to step out by faith.

DOORWAYS to Greater Faith

We also see that faith does, indeed, prove itself. It is something that proves its own reality. As Jesus speaks to the sick man: *"Get up, pick up your bed and go home."* The paralytic obeys and goes home, healed and forgiven. Do not be intimidated by anything, ever! Come to Jesus boldly. This is Jesus' fourth teaching on faith.✝

Study Questions:

1. Have you ever felt that Jesus was too busy for you to express your needs to Him?
2. What might such a thought be expressing about your faith?
3. Is there anything in your personality that is preventing your faith from being stronger?
4. What kind of things or what situations in life stunt your faith? Have things happened to you that you need to approach Jesus about?
5. How can you build up your own persistence in practicing your faith? What new patterns or habits do you need to develop?

CHAPTER 5

FAITH TOUCHES JESUS
Matthew 9:20-22

How often the desperate person overlooks Jesus. Yet, the Bible uses everything from sickness, to storms, to demonic spirits, to death, to miracles, to reveal that God can and does meet every desperate need when we reach to Him in faith.

The news of this wonder is so needed; three gospels lift up this story of Jesus meeting the need of this one particular woman with a history of hemorrhaging. Mark 5:25-34 and Luke 8:43-48 used the event of the Gerasene Demoniac as an introduction while speaking of Jesus' Faith-Forming teaching. Jesus wants us to know we should expect Him to meet us in our desperation; that He is present and able, always. Each time this story of the woman with the issue of blood is shared, it is preceded by references to the death of the synagogue official's daughter and the authority of Jesus in bringing her back to life. The point is Jesus wants us aware that we should expect the new life of faith to change us, to make us new — changed and whole. The woman with the issue of blood faces a serious problem that had already robbed her of life and would probably eventually have caused her death. Certainly, continuous hemorrhaging for twelve years had left her weak and sickly and without energy.

In this life, where we rub elbows with others, situations can become overwhelming. Those things that break down society, distress and disturb, that try to steal our joy, are meant to tear us away from our Lord and the fullness of life we have been provided through faith in Him. The truth is that for our faith to continue on in the strengthening process, we must allow nothing to interfere with us reaching through and touching through to Jesus' heart. Jesus wants these truths to become normal for us earth dwellers. This hemorrhaging and dying woman is a picture of how we must reach out to Jesus with all abandon. It doesn't matter what people think of us. Everyone shunned this woman because she was unclean. Anyone she touched would have been considered unclean. She reached beyond the seemingly insurmountable boundaries to touch the hem of the garment of her Savior, and Jesus responded to her unwavering faith. Imagine living the life of a person rejected by all. You are alone with no accepting face around you, all are careful to stay away from you. By law, you are actually mandated to stay

> *The miracles that Jesus did were to show us the same kind of miracles we can expect Him to do in and around us today.*

5: FAITH TOUCHES JESUS

away from everyone else because of your sickness. The shunning of a person, in such a cruel manner, would have a horrific effect on their attitude about life and others. You would think this woman would have held out no hope after twelve long years.

She had tried everything. Doctors had only caused her more suffering. Every effort to help caused her to get worse. All her resources depleted on doctors and other efforts to get well, her life is nearly blotted out. Along comes Jesus. She hears of Him. She knew this man healed and made people new. That very moment a large crowd was closely following Him and pressing in on Him (Mark 5:24). The mission Jesus was on was to raise to life the dead twelve-year old daughter of the synagogue official.

Press on that you may lay hold of that for which Christ laid hold of you.

We have already seen how this authority in Jesus grants great boldness. Authority often looks like "hope for me" to onlookers. Hebrews 11:1 calls it, *"faith that is the assurance or substance of the things one hopes for... the evidence of things unseen."* Jesus must have looked so unreachable, in the center of that pressing crowd, that she felt she did not have the right to even approach. Yet faith rose up within her as she saw Him. Everyone had heard of the wonders this man performed. Her hope increased even further as she forged ahead. Oh, if only she could touch Him. Her need and hope stirred her to greater boldness. Then, her heart cried out, *"If I only touch His garment, I will get well!"* Matthew 9:21. Luke, the physician, said she pressed up behind Jesus, and stretched out and touched His

DOORWAYS to Greater Faith

garment. Instantly her hemorrhaging stopped. Although Jesus had not seen her, He was instantly aware when she touched Him — aware that power went out from Him in response to the enormous faith she exhibited in that touch (Luke 8:46).

"'Who is the one who touched Me?' Jesus asks" (Luke 8:45).

The disciples point out the obvious. Everyone is touching Him in the thick and pressing crowd. There are nine different words for "*touch*" in the Greek language, each with a different meaning. There is a touch that means to lead another, another touch that means around or concerning, another means to feel the surface of, and yet another one means to alter or manipulate another. The word for "*touch*" that Jesus used when He asked, "*Who touched Me?*" means, "*to fasten upon or to light up or kindle a fire.*" It is a self-conscious effort to reach out and touch through to Jesus.

Jesus is aware when any person touches Him with prayer. Power goes forth and it kindles a fire in Jesus and us.

You see, there are those who touch Jesus in impersonal ways and, then there are those who touch Him in personal ways. Jesus wanted to know who touched through to the fire of His heart, to the fire of His power. Who really wanted Him? Who was reaching out? What is so intriguing about this is He knew who touched Him. Mark 5:32 reads: "*And He looked around to see the woman who had done this.*" There is never a moment when Jesus Christ is not fully aware of what *you* are doing toward Him. His questions are usually His way of teaching, causing us to look within and see what we are doing with Him so we can turn our attention back on Him. When Jesus looked around to see her, she came forward and fell down be-

5: FAITH TOUCHES JESUS

fore Him telling Him the whole truth. In Jesus' timely question, we see the teaching of faith-formation that is directed to the crowd and to His disciples. He knows when you touch Him. Then Jesus calls her, "*daughter.*" He claims her, giving her a sense of belonging. This rejected, unloved, unwanted woman finally found acceptance. "*Daughter, your faith has made you well; go in peace*" (Luke 8:48). Peace? What a wonderful gift! Along with her healing, the Lord gives her something additional that she has not experienced for twelve years.

Jesus demonstrates another step in firming up and strengthening the believer's faith. Wherever we are, and whatever is going on around us, regardless of what others have done to us, or whatever we have accepted of what others have done, there is a point in faith when we can push through anyway, and trust Jesus. No one else will or can do it for you. Others can throw up all kinds of positive or negative interference, but trusting people's voices, good or bad, can actually hinder a person's faith. Look to Jesus! We can also touch Jesus with a desperate heart that pays no attention to the erroneous traditions we've learned from man. We can touch Him with a heart that knows He and He alone will and can meet our deepest need. He alone knows those deepest needs. We can touch Him with a heart that will continue to press through. This is what touches the heart of Jesus. Ultimately, like the healed woman, when we find Jesus, we find peace as well. We no longer depend upon our own selves for peace of mind, but on a truer and higher source.

> *Your faith, like Jesus' faith as a man, is living in the assurance that God absolutely will fulfill every promise and word that He has spoken.*

Jesus compared that kind of heart touching to a man so caught up in a woman that he leaves his parents and is joined to his woman in marriage (Ephesians 5:31,32). The heart we have toward Jesus runs after Him with all abandon. He said marriage is an example to us of who Christ is to the Church. In other words, this is the faith we have found in Him. Reach to Jesus with that kind of total heart-reach. This is the next Faith-Forming step Jesus reveals to His disciples and to the rest of us.
✝

Study Questions:

1. A believer is a new creature. What newness have you experienced to this stage in your growing faith?
2. What do you think is your next step in allowing God to transform you into a new creature?
3. Have you felt shunned at times by other people? Do you feel accepted by Jesus?
4. Have you recognized your situations and troubled times as opportunities from God to teach you to start reaching out to touch Jesus?
5. When studying with others, discuss the truths that are being revealed to you, personally, in these chapters. How is your growth in faith related to your relationship with Jesus?

CHAPTER 6

FAITH HAS NO BRAKES
Matthew 14:13–33

It takes serious boldness to drive a car down the road with no brakes. Imagine that! This is exactly what God wants us to do with our faith. We are to get in the car and set it in gear and never look back. We don't need brakes. We don't need to steer. Have you ever seen the bumper sticker that says, "God is my co-pilot." Well, folks, God should be your pilot! You should be sitting in the passenger seat. That is a perfect picture of faith with no brakes.

> *Expect Jesus to be extravagant in the faith teaching circumstances He puts in your life.*

Jesus drove with no brakes, too. Here He drives right into supernatural activity. After ministering for several hours, the multitude of five thousand men, plus women and children grew hungry. In answer to the need, Jesus sends the disciples on a search for groceries. Five loaves and two fish were found, the lunch of a small boy, and brought to Jesus. He looked up to heaven and blessed the food.

Heads up, there's more. Jesus never uses the brakes. With His perpetual forward momentum, He first healed the sick; then He fed multitudes with five loaves and two fish until they were filled; last, He has the leftovers collected. There is much to be learned from this collection — which is often overlooked. In another chapter, we will look at the wonder of this collection and more about this miracle in greater depth.

Our faith will not be bound by the familiar when we remember we have an extravagant God. He loves to do more than we expect. Let us be bold enough to accept this truth, and therefore, be willing to open our minds and hearts to a God who works above our expectations. He is God, yes, and He will bless our faith.

> *Our thoughts and attitudes have the ability to block our minds to God and His words to us or to free and open our minds to God.*

That is why our action to believe is so important! That's also why the Lord reminds us of His supernatural extravagance as we study this next faith-forming teaching. Jesus does these things to encourage us to be expectant concerning anything He decides to do. We are to be a willing and believing people. The stage is set for faith. Immediately after the miracle of loaves and fishes and their multiplication, Jesus sent the disciples ahead of Him in a boat, then sent the crowds away. He then went up on the mountain to ask the Father what was the next thing He wanted Jesus to do (Matthew 14:22-33). Asking God what He wants is a great way to start our walk of faith each

6: FAITH HAS NO BRAKES

day. Jesus did this continually. In this, we see Jesus' own faith in the will of God as He went off by Himself to pray quite often.

Suddenly, Jesus brings them into yet another faith-stretching situation disguised as another problem in everyday life. The boat the disciples were on was battered by the wind and waves. Notice that Jesus had sent them into this very situation. They were in total obedience.

Sometime after 3 a.m., Jesus comes to them, walking on the water (Matthew 14:25). Prior to this event, the disciples had been rowing to stay in the same place for hours while Jesus is up on the mountain, praying. They were in a tough situation and Jesus was off in His prayer room. We may think this a bit absurd. Let's check out the situation. Mark 6:47 tells us that Jesus sent the disciples away in the boat much earlier in the day because by the evening, the boat was in the middle of the sea. Now Jesus comes walking on the water. By that time, the disciples had rowed, almost in the same place, for some nine or more hours. They had to be exhausted. We can be sure that some time during that long prayer vigil Jesus prayed for the disciples. He does the same for us. In John 17, we read of Jesus praying for both His disciples and for us, as well.

The disciples, rowing against the raging sea, were about to see Peter do a supernatural wonder through faith in Jesus. Peter had to step out in obedience to exercise his faith in order to experience the miracle of walking on the water along with Jesus. The disciples saw Jesus walking on the water and were terrified and cried out in fear, thinking He was a ghost. Jesus immediately said, "Take *courage, it is I; do not be afraid"* (Matthew 14:27). An important factor to recognize here is the effect that fear has on our minds. It is an emotion that blocks our minds, and often paralyzes not only the thoughts, but the body, too. Such an emotional state has the ability to cancel faith in a person. It can block God's will out completely. The Bible tells us that we have not been given a spirit of fear, but of power, love and a sound mind. Fear is not of God. The absence of fear, then, opens the mind to receive God's peace. Jesus immediately spoke to the situation by saying, *"Take courage, it is I (I Am!); do not be afraid."* This is a continuous command for us as we walk out this life in faith, so it stands for us, too. The person of faith is commanded to grant no entrance to fear. It is inconsistent with faith. Repeatedly the Bible tells us to, *"Fear not!"*

> *Simply put, faith believes and fear does not believe.*

A second meaning of the Greek word for faith is to *trust*. To trust God is to fear not. To fear or be terrified greatly hampers what faith can accomplish. Simply put, faith believes and fear does not believe. Fear and faith cannot coexist.

Calming one's fear is accomplished by trusting Jesus, not by some self-action like turning up one's boldness. This, also, is a step in the strengthening of one's faith. Notice that even the disciples needed to learn this. They were present with Jesus on this earth, saw His wonderful miracles, yet still had to learn not to respond to the emotion of fear and allow it to rule their lives. Never be discouraged by being fearful.

There is a measure or type of fear that God has instilled in us as a built-in safety feature. It keeps your fingers off the hot stove! We are to look to Jesus when fear begins to stir. Also,

6: FAITH HAS NO BRAKES

learn to use your legs if you need to get away. Jesus will tell you which to do. Be bold with Jesus in each situation He allows in your life. Be assured that there is a reason for the situations God allows in our lives.

As soon as Jesus said, *"It is I,"* which is, *"I Am,"* in Greek and is the identifying name of God in the Old Testament, the disciples immediately became calm. At that point, Peter grew bold in his faith. He said, *"Lord, if it is You, command me to come to You on the water"* (Matthew 14:28). Peter's boldness in Christ springs up. We are all encouraged to be bold in using faith in the same way in our lives. Peter understood the authority of Jesus. He had learned of it in some of Jesus' first teachings on faith. He knew if Jesus commanded him to do a thing, Peter could do it. Jesus commanded: *"Come!"* Peter got out of the boat and walked toward Jesus. He did not think of the pros and cons of obeying. He simply acted. To think of the adverse possibilities is to invite doubt. James 1:7 tells us if we doubt, we should not expect to receive anything from the Lord. Peter ex-

> *Your faith, whatever its size, is enough for you to do anything Jesus calls you to do.*

pected to receive what Jesus had commanded and that was to *"come"* to Him. Peter had faith, believing. This is yet another faith-forming teaching.

Across the water Peter walks. Imagine the wonder of sharing with Jesus in this supernatural activity. At one point, Peter's eyes slipped off Jesus. We are told to run with endurance, the race before us, with our eyes fixed on Jesus. He is the author and perfecter of our faith (Hebrews 12:1-2). Peter's eyes shifted to the storm and waves, and he started sinking. We see

DOORWAYS to Greater Faith

a picture here of Peter, who is off to a great start and full of great faith, suddenly shift to little faith. As one would expect, Jesus rescued him, and right there while walking back toward the boat on Jesus arm, Jesus asked Peter: *"Oh, you of little faith, why did you doubt?"*

Another way to ask the same question that expresses Jesus' thoughts for our generation is: *"Oh, you of little faith, why didn't you continue what you started?"*

This faith-forming teaching tells us not to allow fear to shift our focus. The storm looked ominous and Peter began to fear he would sink and drown. He shifted his gaze from the eyes of Jesus and put them on the object of his fear. Once we respond to Christ's calling, we are to continue in the strong faith with which we started. When God gives us direction, Jesus walks beside us and the Holy Spirit guides us. Let us continue what *we* started. God assures us that with faith, we have all the resources to do so.‡

Study Questions:

1. How do you seek the will of God in your life?
2. Will you commit to spending some time to find God's will in your life by reading and praying and asking for direction?
3. What is the best way you've found to keep your eyes on Jesus?
4. How do you guard your mind from fearful thoughts?

6: FAITH HAS NO BRAKES

5. What do you do to correct those "little faith" words that slip out at unexpected moments, those words that are edifying to no one? See Ephesians 4:29.
6. Have you continued in the faith with which you started ? Peter didn't, but he could have. He could have walked all the way to the shore. Will you?

CHAPTER

7

FAITH PRESSES ON
Matthew 15:21–28

Earlier in the Gospels, Jesus laid the foundation concerning who He is and the practice of faith-forming. He laid the foundations so soundly that in Matthew 15:21–28 it reached into the Gentile world. In the very next chapter, Matthew 16:16, Peter says to Jesus, "*You are the Christ, the Son of the living God.*" Jesus tells him he is blessed because flesh and blood could not have revealed that kind of truth to Peter, but the Father who is in heaven did. The disciples had grown greatly in faith. However, being human, there is always room for growth in faith until we see the Lord in eternity. Never be satisfied with where you are in faith. When Paul had almost reached the end of his ministry, after serving the Lord for twenty-five or more years, he said in Philippians 3:12–14 that he had not attained the goal he wanted in Christ as yet,

7: FAITH PRESSES ON

but he pressed on that he might lay hold of that for which Christ Jesus laid hold of him. He was still growing in faith. Let us press on; let us also yearn for God.

In Matthew 15:21-28, Jesus had been focused on dealing with Israel, the people and nation through whom God had chosen to give special revelation to the nations. The Canaanites were that evil race of people living in the land that God had promised to Abraham. In the Old Testament the name Canaan was used to refer to all of the people of the area we call Palestine, which is located west of the Jordan. In Biblical times, it also included the Amorites. Referring to these peoples, Genesis 15:16 speaks of the iniquity of the Amorites (Canaanites) as not being complete. When the sin of this people was complete, she would be destroyed (Numbers 21:1-3). Also, see Exodus 23:28-33. Here is a Canaanite woman who comes to Jesus, an evil race that was an enemy of the Israelites.

However, the Canaanite woman in Matthew 15 has faith. Faith makes anyone acceptable to Jesus. Faith gains God's approval because we are told that without faith it is impossible to please God. (Hebrews 11:2). We are told that God so loved the world He gave His Son. Yes, and God so loves the world anyone can have great faith. Even we can. Even you can! The Canaanite woman came to Jesus crying out, *"Have mercy on me, Lord, Son of David; my daughter is cruelly demon-possessed"* (Matthew 15:22).

As we follow this historical account, remember how Jesus wouldn't even speak to this woman! He didn't say a word. The disciples even joined in, not understanding what Jesus was doing, and they begged Jesus to send her away; "Send *her away, because she keeps shouting at us"* (Matthew 15:23). Perhaps, as some think, Jesus was educating her faith. It was not right for a Canaanite to put herself forward as if she were an Israelite by calling Jesus the Son of David. Some believe the title, Son of David, was a title for use only by the Jews. We call Jesus by that name today — we, the sons of Abraham — through our own faith. I think Jesus was setting the stage, getting the disciples involved so they would not forget this teaching on faith — who Jesus is to us and how faith reaches beyond the boundaries of all worldly situations and thought processes.

Finally, Jesus did speak to her: *"I was sent only to the lost sheep of the house of Israel."* In Jesus' unresponsiveness at first, this Canaanite woman didn't act like many of us do when we feel Jesus has ignored us. We get angry. We start accusing, we who are counted as faithful. Picture us coming in prayer before God's throne, shouldering past the four living creatures standing there day and night, who do not cease saying forever: "**Holy,** HOLY, Holy... *is the Lord God, the Almighty, who was and who is and who is to come"* (Revelation 4:8). Picture us pressing past these creatures, in their focused worship. We angrily march up to God's throne and accuse Him, in our misunderstanding of His work, as He seeks to make us more like Jesus. It is right to express our feelings toward God, but there should quickly come a time of confession as we come to an understanding of what God is doing. Because of His great love that He lavishes upon us, we know He's doing what's good for us. He is doing what is absolutely best for us!

This woman recognized the power and love in Jesus. She bowed at His feet, saying, *"Lord, help me!"* The word *worship*

7: FAITH PRESSES ON

when interpreted in this verse means: *"bowed at His feet."* It literally means to *kiss, to adore.* Some have translated the word *worship* as meaning, *"to kiss the face of God."* This Canaanite woman had a healthy and reverent attitude. The Greek tense here literally draws a picture of her in continual worship. She adored Him. She had come for the sake of her demon-possessed daughter.

This kind of power and love happened to my wife and me one time. I dropped to my knees and all I could pray was "Lord, Help!" Before I got the second word, "Help" out of my mouth, the atmosphere of the room felt thick as God's presence permeated the room and His peace flooded over us before I could finish the word. God is present always and on time with what we need. As my wife and I needed help at that very moment, He showed up as we worshipped Him. Jesus hadn't finished His teaching on faith yet for the disciples. He told the Canaanite woman, *"It is not good to take the children's bread and throw it to the dogs."* As it is used here, *"dog"* here means a *little dog,* and it refers to the impurities and abominations of heathens. It is not with the intention of demeaning the pets in our families that are "man's best friend," but Jesus was making a very belittling statement here. It was not one made out of being harsh, but one to test her pride. Jesus will do this with us at times — and they will be times when we are beaten and bruised and we will have no pride left. This is usually the time when we are most willing to obey and trust God. This is usually the time when our worship is most pure. She refused to be discouraged, no matter what. She pressed in to Him and did not deny her unworthiness. She was an unworthy sinner like the rest of us. What she wanted was healing for her daughter, and I believe Jesus was also touched by her unselfish sacrifice to press in through the crowd in spite of circumstance and fight for someone else's benefit.

Faith, of this caliber is awesome before God. Mixed with knowing who Jesus is, faith is irresistible to God and it holds to the truth; it leads one to worship and adore Him. The answer from this unwelcomed woman is this: *"Yes, Lord; but even the dogs feed on the crumbs which fall from their master's table."* She knew to whom she was speaking — her Lord. When He had fully tested her, Jesus lets His emotions of love and acceptance for this woman flood over her. *"O woman, your faith is great; it shall be done for you as you wish."* Her daughter was healed at once. During His ministry, Jesus said only two people had great faith, and both were Gentiles: This Canaanite woman and the Roman centurion commander we spoke of earlier.

Here is what we have learned about the growth and forming of our faith: The first part of this faith-forming lesson in this chapter is the faith that Jesus calls, *"great faith."* Great faith is persistent. We are to continue steadily and firmly, pressing into God with our faith as we approach Him. The second lesson here is that faith takes whatever God says as He corrects us, even when He speaks things that could cause us to stumble. Faith presses on worshipping and adoring and trusting God anyway.

Faith knows that whatever God says or does is for our growth and He is always testing us to increase our faith. God knows that it is by faith that we will live this life in the manner which He has prepared for us. ☨

7: FAITH PRESSES ON

STUDY QUESTIONS:

1. How would you define your persistence?
2. Are you satisfied with your heart of worship?
3. What would you do, and why, if for any reason you thought Jesus said or thought negative things about you? Remember that the things God allows in your life He uses for the very best for you.
4. Has God ever tested your faith?
5. If so, what was the test? What was your response?

CHAPTER 8

FAITH REMEMBERS JESUS' WORKS
Matthew 16:5-12

We find Jesus' next teaching on faith in Matthew 16:5-12. The disciples were maturing more than they realized in the Faith-Forming School of Jesus. We sense they had been maturing because we see an example eight verses later, in verse 16, after Jesus had called them, "*men of little faith,*" Peter confesses, "You *are the Christ, the Son of the living God.*" Such a confession is a high point of faith. Notice how their hearts seem to leap back and forth much as ours do at times. One day they seem to have little faith, and then days later, they exhibit great faith. We have all faced the same inconsistencies at times.

Jesus and the disciples arrived in the region of Magadan on the western shore of the Sea of Galilee after another boat ride. They must have arrived while still discussing the miracle

8: FAITH REMEMBERS JESUS' WORK

they had just seen. Jesus had fed another crowd of four thousand men, plus women and children by multiplying seven loaves and a few small fish. (Matthew 15:38).

Remember that when Jesus fed the five thousand, plus women, and children the Apostle John said the five barley loaves and two fish were the lunch of a small lad (John 6:9). We get a good picture here of the wonder of the work Jesus did through His own faith. Jesus started with very little and allowed God to multiply it, having faith that God would do according to Jesus' faith. This miracle is not just an imagined story or fable as the world would have us think. God is able to provide in wonderful ways, and He does!

> *Our human inadequacy is no excuse when Jesus has sent the Holy Spirit and promised to be our strength in all of our weaknesses.*

As we guard our minds and the truth of God's Word, we must be careful about what we think and what we say. Our words have a way of finding their mark, good or bad. When our thoughts or words contradict Scriptural truth, we negate what God's Word says. We see examples of this in the way Jesus guarded Himself when He was tempted in Matthew 4:1–10. Each time the tempter spoke to Jesus, to influence Jesus' thoughts, Jesus quoted the Bible to replace the tempter's incorrect manipulations of God's Word. Jesus kept His mind full of the Father's accurate teachings.

We need to think as absolute as God does when it comes to faith. We have a supernatural God who is limited to help us only as much as our belief system allows. Jesus' activity, as He worked in faith, is what God had always planned to be normal

DOORWAYS to Greater Faith

activity for mankind. The Bible teaches us that, as a man, Jesus was only exercising the same faith that God expects every believer to exercise. Jesus even told us that because of the power of the Holy Spirit He would send to us, we would be able to do more! As you read the Book of Acts and about the church's history, you see acts of faith exhibited by our predecessors. God is about answering your own prayers. It's important that we never forget how Jesus had laid aside His privileges as God (Phil 2:7), so that God might demonstrate in Jesus the kind of faith-life He calls us to live.

> *We need to know and remember that the supernatural is present in us right now.*

The disciples were distracted upon arriving in this new region by some Pharisees and Sadducees who were apparently testing Jesus. Afterward, when Jesus told the disciples to beware of the leaven of the teachings of the Pharisees and Sadducees, they errantly thought He was correcting them for forgetting to bring along some of the leftover bread from feeding the four thousand. It is easy to be distracted from the accurate teachings of Jesus. We have all read the Bible or listened to teachings only to later discover our minds were focused elsewhere. Distractions can clip the wings of faith and even keep us from God's purpose for our lives. Here we see distraction turn the disciples down a road they had no need to travel in their thoughts. They missed the lesson as their attention seemed not to be fixed on their Teacher.

Have we noticed that in every case, what we bring to the Lord is very small and inadequate compared to His power and glory? With Jesus and His great faith, a small lad's lunch

8: FAITH REMEMBERS JESUS' WORK

was more than ample to feed the five thousand and the lad received more back than he gave. Stop and consider this for a moment. Strong faith makes us aware that we have an extravagant God. He takes our small faith and multiplies the result with His supernatural extravagant love for us!

The disciples found themselves in school again and again. Jesus called them men of little faith because they were not trusting in His ability and willingness to supply their need. *"Don't you understand what I have been doing,"* Jesus asked? *"Do you not yet understand or remember the five loaves of the five thousand, and how many baskets full you picked up? Or the seven loaves of the four thousand, and how many large baskets full you picked up?"* See Matthew 16:9-10. The word *"understand"* means to *"call to mind."* It is expressed in a tense that means to continuously call to mind the things Jesus had done with them. In other words, believers are often so distracted by cares and their human inadequacies that they do not remember all that God has already done in and through them. Our human inadequacy is no excuse when Jesus has promised to be our strength in all of our weaknesses. All we need do is believe and act on our belief in Jesus Christ.

I remember once while I was out making house calls, the Lord suddenly said, *"Go home now!"* Did I hear a voice? I don't know, but I knew in my spirit I was supposed to go home at that very moment! *"Go home now!"* It was an inner voice that could not be denied or ignored. I turned without giving it a second thought and headed for home as fast as I could. When I was almost home, this same voice rose in my spirit, *"Turn here!"* It was the longer route, and I had questions, but I obeyed the voice and turned. Going around a curve, there I saw my own two small children trying to hold their bikes between themselves and a vicious German Shepherd that was attacking them. I was called there to rescue the children. I did.

Another time, while in seminary, our monthly heating bill was due. In those days, our bill was rather small, but for us it seemed like two thousand dollars. Since we had nothing, we did not have the money to pay it! The bill was for thirteen dollars and twenty-seven cents. It was the middle of winter and our heat was about to be turned off. We prayed together, "Lord, we need thirteen dollars and twenty-seven cents." The next day we opened the mailbox to find a check for thirteen dollars and twenty-seven cents. Where did the money come from? Fifteen months before that, we had sold our car so we could attend seminary in New York City. Our car insurance company had somehow discovered that we had sold our car and they had been searching for our address so they could send a refund for the policy as we no longer needed it. The timing of this was a miracle and a perfect answer to our prayer. We realized that God had prepared to answer our prayer fifteen months prior to our need. We did not even think of asking any person for help. We just asked the Lord to meet our need. We have trusted God, and He comes through each and every time.

There have been several such signs of God's presence and power in our home and church. Once, the parents of a deaf infant asked the elders of our church to pray for the child's healing. Two doctors and a hearing clinic had said the infant was completely deaf. The infant never looked at anyone unless

8: FAITH REMEMBERS JESUS' WORK

they were in the range of his vision. He never responded to loud noises. As we began praying, suddenly the child, for the first time, jerked and began to look back over his head, then forward toward whoever was praying. This child was healed immediately! Other examples of God's miracles have occurred in our church and in individual lives. I believe each of us as Christians, who believe in God and not coincidence, has known and seen similar things.

The main teaching to remember here is that we are to call to mind our past experiences of those times when Jesus revealed His power to us, in us and through us. We are to recall them, *remember* them, and allow Jesus to help us understand the meaning of those experiences of His power as we walk through today's time of testing. We have the memory of miracles, those things He has already done. Like the Israelites walking through the desert toward the Promised Land, we are to remember how God parts the Red Sea in our lives!

STUDY QUESTIONS:

1. What is behind the disciples' need in this chapter?
2. What are the implications of their actions in not remembering or understanding what Jesus had done in the past?
3. What changes in our patterns and habits should we make in our actions as they exercise fear or faith? Who or what contributes to your old patterns of doubt and fear?

4. How do you view the possibility of miracles in your life as Jesus is a part of your daily life and wants to be there for you? In what ways have you seen God provide?
5. What attributes of God and the active and faithful believer are emphasized in this study?

CHAPTER

FAITH IS A PERSONAL RELATIONSHIP
Matthew 17:14-21

As the disciples traveled with Jesus, they had been growing in Jesus' School of Faith-Forming. They still had a lot to learn about what Jesus being the Messiah meant for them and their faith, just as we have much to learn. As we have noted before, it is a continual process. A greater awareness is present in the disciples now. In Matthew 16:16, Peter confesses, *"You are the Christ, the Son of the living God."*

This confession was like an announcement of the disciple's personal growth in their relationship to Jesus. They know Him! We are even told, in Matthew 17:19, of the disciples feeling free to come to Jesus privately to find why they could not drive the demon out of a boy. God always wants us to see Him as a personal Father. The disciples were learning this importance as they walked close to Jesus daily.

DOORWAYS to Greater Faith

Before this, God had come to them through Jesus to teach them of His love. Jesus had urged, *"Come to Me, all who are weary and heavy-laden ... take My yoke ... learn from Me ... I am gentle ... you will find rest for your soul ... My burden is light"* (Matthew 11:28-30).

God is concerned for each of us. God wants each of us to draw near to Him. God cares about our daily burdens. God is willing to work with each of us, individually. He is gentle. God will give rest to our souls, the place where we are most aware of ourselves — the place where He is aware of us. God's burden is not too heavy for us. God cannot say it any more clearly as He wants us all to fully understand His love and concern for us each moment we exist. He wants to impress upon us that He most sincerely desires our close fellowship. You are important to God. God knows us at the core of our hearts, problems and all, and this is what Almighty God created us to be — His companions. The disciples finally understand. He *is* the Son of the living God, the Christ. This understanding is something so paramount to the power exhibited by Jesus and now it is available to them... and to us!

We see this revelation and understanding revealed in their new activity and actions. For instance, Peter knew that, at least, this meant that what the Lord instructed him to do he could certainly do it. There is the event of Peter raising Tabitha to life in Acts. 9:40. He didn't do as we might do. When we are asked to pray, we often launch ourselves into prayer. Peter was more sensitive to the will of God. He was coming to Jesus, reaching out and touching Him, paying no attention to his own limitations, pressing on into Jesus, perhaps remembering

9: FAITH IS A PERSONAL RELATIONSHIP

his walk on the water, and understanding the will of God, which is to help others. He knelt by Tabitha's dead body, already washed and prepared for the grave, and prayed to the gentle One for instruction. Then, having received from God what He wanted Peter to do, Peter quit praying, turned to Tabitha's body and commanded: "Tabitha, arise!" He commanded Tabitha, speaking life into her through God's instructions that he had received when he prayed.

Consider this. In Matthew 18:18, all believers are told that whatever they bind on earth shall have been bound in heaven, and whatever they loose on earth shall be loosed in heaven. That authority belongs to every Christian. John said all who receive Jesus; to them He gives the right, the authority, to become children of God. That word for authority, *exousia*, means the same thing for us that it meant for Jesus when He was in the flesh of man. It means *"an authority that denies the presence of any hindrance"* when God instructs you as to what you should do. Jesus had taught the disciples that they would have to take up their cross. We must do the same! Simply put, we are to live in surrender to God's will. We believers are called to live not for us, but for God. This is called obedience, and we are told in the Bible that obedience means more to God than anything we could sacrifice (I Samuel 15:22). Obedience implies a relationship with God that enables hearing His guidance. We are His children. As we obey, we see the goodness of God and His power.

Now, notice how we tend to drift. Matthew 17:1 says Jesus takes Peter, James, and John up on a high mountain by themselves and is transfigured before them. He shone like the sun

DOORWAYS to Greater Faith

with dazzling brilliance, from the inside out. His brightness even caused His clothes to shine (Matthew 17:2). The disciples see Jesus' glory and wanted to settle down right where they were on this great revelation and build three tabernacles. We want to continue to revel in our initial supernatural experience with God when we surrendered our lives to Him rather than move forward with Him and experience continued supernatural growth. We tend to want to settle down and stop growing when we receive some insight or experience, some revival or other power of Jesus. We want to stop right there. While we can praise God and be thankful for the wonderful things He has done, God wants us to go on growing and learning and having intimate, personal fellowship with Him.

Our call is not to settle down in past experiences of our Lord. We are to move forward, growing, learning and having fellowship.

God interrupted the thoughts the three disciples were having at His transfiguration and said, "*This is My beloved Son, with whom I am well-pleased; listen to Him!*" They were terrified. Jesus immediately touched them and told them to guard their thoughts, and to, "*Get up, and do not be afraid*" (Matthew 17:7).

The three disciples got up, looked around, and saw that Moses and Elijah, who had been talking with Jesus were no longer there. Only Jesus was left. He wanted them to know His relationship would continue as it does for you and me. When all else is gone, we will always have Jesus. He assured us, in His departing words, that He would always be with us.

This next teaching on faith-forming becomes clear when, regardless of the things Jesus had been revealing to the disci-

9: FAITH IS A PERSONAL RELATIONSHIP

ples in the past few days, they could not cure a man's son who had a demon in him (Matthew 17:14-18). The demon was causing the child to have epilepsy. According to Mark 9:18, the child was foaming at the mouth.

Imagine the thoughts of the people present as Jesus looking at His disciples and the crowd said, *"You unbelieving and perverted generation, how long shall I be with you? How long shall I put up with you? Bring him here to Me"* (Matthew 17:17). We are like the disciples who wanted to know why they couldn't drive the demon out.

This next thing He said is an unexpected revelation Jesus had been moving toward from the beginning of His teaching. *"Truly I say to you, if you have faith the size of a mustard seed, you will say to this mountain, 'Move from here to there,' and it will move; and nothing will be impossible to you"* (Matthew 17:20b).

For years, I thought a mustard seed was the size of that mustard seed we see in a jar of sweet pickles. What I found out is that, if we want to know the size of a mustard seed, we need to shake some finely ground black pepper on a piece of white paper. The smallest flicks of pepper are the size of that mustard seed Jesus was speaking about, and the tree from this tiny seed grows as high as a two-story house.

The point Jesus makes here is that the tiniest speck of faith works. So you, dear believer, have nothing to worry about concerning your faith. Jesus said a fleck of faith makes everything possible. Jesus said: *"All things are possible to him who believes"* (Mark 9:23). He also promises to give us the measure of faith we need to do what He asks us to do. Listen, here is a wonder we are missing! Primarily, God sent Jesus to save us.

Then He sent the Spirit to empower us. To have faith in God is to have faith that He is able. God has also promised that for Him, nothing is impossible. With all of these promises, what have we to fear? With a little faith and all of God we walk in complete wholeness. With Jesus and the Holy Spirit, God supplies all of our needs.

Though we do not have to be concerned about the size of our faith, it is important to God that our faith and relationship with Him continues to grow. God's goal is for us to move into a personal relationship with Him and to be drawing ever near to Him. Over and over again the Bible teaches that God wants your whole heart. As we would give our hearts to God, He wants our hearts to desire Him even more than we desire our beloved spouses and/or earthly loved ones. This is what it means to truly love God.☦

Study Questions:

1. How do you account for this truth, that all things are possible for you through faith?
2. How important is hearing God's instructions before you pray for others? Do you spend time alone with God so you know His voice?
3. Listening for God's instructions before we pray is crucial. How can we increasingly make this truth known and practiced among praying people?
4. Knowing that your heart includes your will, desire, time and focus, how are you giving your heart to God?

CHAPTER 10

FAITH MOVES BEYOND THE ORDINARY
Matthew 21:18-22

Faith is ever blossoming, ever growing. There is no stopping place for the growth of faith. The quality of the *"nothing will be impossible for you"* kind of faith is so important to understand that Jesus repeated it in Matthew 21:18-22.

On His way to Jerusalem, Jesus went to a fig tree to find fruit for breakfast. The tree should have had ripe figs because it was in leaf. Fig trees either bear figs just before leafing or both figs and leaves can appear together. In either case, figs should have been ripened and available on the tree. Fig trees in the Mediterranean climate produce fruit early. If no figs were there early it indicated there would be none later on. Jesus therefore said of the fig tree, *"No longer shall there ever be any fruit on you."* The tree immediately withered.

DOORWAYS to Greater Faith

The lesson of the fig tree for Jesus' students is that He is looking for fruit from us, the fruit of His labor and love as we grow in our faith. The last week before going to the cross, Jesus revealed to His disciples that He is the vine, His Father is the vinedresser, and we are the branches that are to bear fruit (John 15:1,2,5).

He comes looking for the fruit on us: Love, joy, peace, longsuffering, gentleness, goodness and yes, you guessed it, faith, along with meekness and temperance (or self control). See Galatians 5:22-23. These things show and tell others what God is doing in us. As we bear fruit, He prunes us so we can bear even more (John 15:2). The pruning activity includes the trials and life situations we often try to pray away before asking the Lord what He wants us to learn from this. If we knew how He is helping us to grow, we might not be so quick to try to pray these things away. In any case, we need to be aware of the purpose of God's work in us as He prunes us through these trials so that we can bear more fruit.

The fig tree event occurs during the last week of Jesus' life. It happened on Sunday. Jesus would be crucified on Friday. Intensive training is occurring here, in Jesus' last hours on Earth, about the things His disciples must retain. One can sense Jesus' urgency by His powerful and no-nonsense teaching, *"Truly I say to you, if you have faith and do not doubt, you will not only do what was done to the fig tree, but even if you say to this mountain, 'Be taken up and cast into the sea,' it will happen. And all things you ask in prayer, believing, you will receive"* (Matthew 21:21–22). What is the definition of *"ask in prayer, believing?"* It is *prayer* after we have determined, by faith, what God will do

10: FAITH MOVES BEYOND THE ORDINARY

in a situation. It is being full of assurance of the Lord's will in a particular prayer situation. The followers of Christ must know about faith, because God's Word declares that the just shall live by faith. This speaks of two kinds of living. One is living in eternity, or eternal life. The other is the living where we are daily — right now in this physical, biological and psychological life. The just, those made righteous by Christ, shall live by faith. The purpose of this book is to define the practices that help open doors of our faith as those practices point us to Jesus in one way or another.

We can presently experience this life of faith in several ways. It can be seen, at times, on the countenance of those who have opened their minds and hearts to receive the gift of faith. It can be felt by others as an out-flowing of peace and power from the Holy Spirit. You have probably felt this before as you have entered a home and perhaps felt peace present in that home. I have heard people exclaim about the peace they feel in a situation where there should be no peace. God is present. The power of one's faith is actually visible in such situations and sets off a yearning in others. The amazing wonder of it is that it is available for all who would receive.

We follow Jesus by deliberately moving forward in our life while choosing to practice the life-style of Jesus Christ.

We all want God-stuff. It is called various things in the Bible. Acts 3:19 calls it, *"refreshing times in the presence of the Lord."* It's called, *"peace, rest, joy,"* even *"completed joy"* in I John 1:4. Jesus said we would live an abundant life, not in terms of finances, but in terms of sheer pleasure of being alive in Jesus

Christ. It is a life released from negative captivity. He also promised us that there would be a recovery of understanding, health and healing both spiritually and physically. We now are able to live a life experiencing God's favor (Luke 4:18-19). Jesus came and gave us the gift of faith for this very reason and for this very season.

We all know there are times when we have not been living this kind of experience. When we miss it, we need to understand that all that can be given has been given and the rest is up to us. He has already handed the gifts to us. *"His divine power has granted to us everything pertaining to life and Godliness through the true knowledge of Him who called us by His own glory and excellence"* (2 Peter 1:3). Perhaps we may have ceased guarding our thoughts and our words that Jesus urges us to guard. When we speak unwholesome words or words that do not edify others, this hampers our ability to respond to Jesus by faith. The faith we have is not lost, but the greater faith we could have is not experienced. We are left poor in faith because of fear and doubt, and also because of spoken words that are contradictory to God's words and thoughts.

The faith-forming teaching for us here is the straightforward truth that if we truly believe, we will be able to do miracles such as Jesus did. Even more, we will be able at Jesus command, to do things as big as moving mountains. We will be able to face any problem if we would have faith in God and do not doubt His providence and His love for us.

Notice how doubt tries try to slip in and destroy our faith. The only thing that can eliminate faith is fear and doubt. We must pay attention to God's supernatural ability to intervene

10: FAITH MOVES BEYOND THE ORDINARY

for us. He knows what He is doing and He knows us. God, through His Spirit, intervenes for us in our need, for He is still the same yesterday, and today, and forever (Hebrews 13:8). We are told to imitate the faith of those who speak the Word of God, referring to what is taught and demonstrated in the Bible (Hebrews 13:7). Remember, the Bible says, call to mind those who led you, who spoke the Word of God to you and imitate their faith.

The Bible is full of the miracles Jesus performed. Though some may think not, we still need the proof of God's miracles in our generation and in all future generations. The Bible tells us that the miracles are not for those who already believe, but to help those who do not believe to see God's power. See Acts 8:6. We know the biblical history about God's wonders over both nature and the spirit world and over life and how He imparts new life in us right now (II Corinthians 5:17). The word "*new,*" is in that verse and means "*a new species never seen or even imagined before.*" Before we forget, we are talking about faith here! Yet some may not be aware that such wonders continued to occur throughout church history. For instance, in 140-202 A.D., Iraneus spoke of visions and healings and deliverances occurring among Christians. St. Basil and Gregory of Nazianzus spoke of the same in 350 A.D. Gregory of Tours in 580 A.D. spoke of a woman paralyzed for 18 years being healed. St. Francis of Assisi in 1200 A.D. spoke of healings occurring. Martin Luther experienced such occurrences in 1530. John Wesley, in 1750, laid hands on a horse and it was healed so he could continue on his journey. People were also healed at his hands of faith. Smith Wigglesworth spoke of such miracles in 1859.

DOORWAYS to Greater Faith

Agnes Sanford, a Southern Presbyterian missionary experienced people being healed instantly in the 1900's. In addition, she was so serious about the power of faith, for the "here and now," that with a group of similar believers they experimented in prayer. Once, to prove the power of faith in prayer, the group prayed concerning a devastating hurricane about to hit the East Coast. They prayed for the hurricane to do an impossible thing — to make a right angle turn out to sea at a particular longitude. It made a right angle turn at the exact place they had prayed for the turning. We, too, can become bold enough to ask God for the extravagant.

> *"By faith" is a way of living that gains God's approval. Jesus marvels when He sees faith in us.*

There are many such illustrations of miracles in the history of the church. You mothers and fathers still pray for your children and each other, and the prayers are answered. Jesus advises us that such experiences need to be remembered and reviewed. You have probably experienced many answered prayers yourself. In answering such prayers, God is feeding your faith so that it will continue to grow. The truths of faith, every one of them, are still true in forming and firming up and strengthening our faith. May God get the praise and may we continue to grow. The faith-forming teaching here is that, as sure as the sun will rise in the morning, if you have faith and do not doubt, you will do the things Jesus did on this earth. Consider how important it is for us Christians to believe our faith can move beyond the ordinary since Jesus emphasized it twice at the end of His ministry on earth.

10: FAITH MOVES BEYOND THE ORDINARY

Remember, in your prayer, how Jesus didn't do anything on His own initiative, but did only what God, His Father, told Him to do and say. In other words, He continually checked in with the Father and was sure that the things He was doing pleased the Father. He, again, was in the direct will and purpose of God. (See John 5:19; John 8:28,29). Jesus calls you to reach out in expectation from where you are now in your faith, and He will move you far beyond the ordinary in your faith life. Be positioned to receive by following God's Word.

God is truly an extravagant God. He wants to show Himself on this earth through you. He can do whatever He chooses, and He has chosen to work through and in you to bring His Word and will to others. When you are positioned to receive, by opening your heart to Him, pray and believe without wavering and you will receive answers to your prayers.

Truly God is extravagant with us, His children. There is even a time coming when those long dead will hear Jesus' voice and live. ☨

STUDY QUESTIONS:

1. Do you believe faith can still move us beyond the ordinary? Share how God has answered prayers in your life.
2. Have you experienced times of refreshing from the Lord? Share some of them.
3. Is it your experience that Christ is the same yesterday and today and forever? Share some ways that God has proven Himself the same as in the Word.

DOORWAYS to Greater Faith

4. Have you experienced anyone being healed or helped through your prayers? As you feel comfortable, share your experiences with others as you study together.
5. Have you seen God increasing your faith? In what ways has God answered the impossible circumstances that you have faced in your life?

Part Two
Facets of Faith

"Now may the God of peace…equip you in every good thing to do His will, working in us that which is pleasing in His sight, through Jesus Christ, to whom be the glory forever and ever. Amen."
(Hebrews 13:20–21)

PART TWO

FACETS OF FAITH

You would correctly expect that faith has many characteristics since it is a spiritual gift from God. We have already discovered in Jesus' multiplication of bread and fish one example of His unlimited abundance. When Jesus multiplied food to feed the crowds, in each miracle much more food was left than that with which He started. Faith is like this in itself. It is unlimited and God will give it to us according to our own acceptance and exercise thereof. It multiplies and is multi-faceted.

I like to think that faith is like a valuable diamond. It has eternal value that gives life and puts pure light on what we see through the eyes of faith. The facets of faith are like the facets of a diamond. Each facet in a diamond is a flat surface, a window, through which light reflects, revealing different qualities of the diamond's beauty. In this study on the facets of faith we will see into the beauty and value of different aspects of faith that are revealed to us.

DOORWAYS to Greater Faith

For instance, we will see that, since the Spirit gives power to the believer through faith, we are filled with boldness to witness to the truth. The place of faith in our lives becomes an area of action where God is present and where He is able to work through the life of the believer. Let us look into these windows and learn of God in these different facets of faith. Let us learn of His work in us through His Spirit from the different facets.

We see many witnesses to these truths in the Bible. We break down Hebrews 11:1 even more: Faith is defined as the *assurance or substance of things hoped for and the conviction or evidence of things not seen as yet.* Since substance is also matter, the materials of the physical creation, we also understand that faith is the "spiritual matter" of things produced in our lives in the spiritual realm. One more facet of faith, then, is that it gives the believer foundational building blocks for God's plan and frees us from limitations.

Faith gives the believer foundational building blocks for God's plan and frees us from limitations.

These limitations are those we come to accept when we see ourselves as merely biological beings. God created us in His image, therefore, we already possess what God has given us by faith. We are spiritual beings, and our responsibility is, by faith, to begin taking possession of the fullness of our gift of faith. Interestingly, when we take hold of our faith, we let go of ourselves, completely.

Faith does its work in our spiritual being and brings the biological being, in line with God's truth. Being the new creatures that we are, John 1:12 says we have authority to become

PART TWO — FACETS OF FAITH

children of God. Children of God are we who are surrendered to the will of God, who then yearn to fulfill the purpose for which God created us. Christ becomes our life, and as we surrender to His guidance, all things are now possible. This is because God Himself is working through us. The Word says that nothing is impossible for God. Therefore, as we are filled with the Spirit of God, nothing is impossible for us!

Now, in obedience to God, we are to give up all claims we previously had on our own lives and choose to let Jesus use our bodies here on earth. Let us yield to His creative work in us. Then, we can walk in bold faith, being steadfast in our knowledge of His love and His power that works within us. Our task is to continually be learning and forging ahead by faith in Jesus Christ. He taught us certain practices in His Faith-Forming School that help us know and trust Him so that our faith rises up and He is able to work His wonders through us.

Jesus spoke of the limitations and dangers of having any part of our lives rooted back in the world's ways. Jesus makes a simple statement of three words in Luke 17:32: *"Remember Lot's wife,"* referencing us back to Genesis 19:26 where she looked back on God's destruction of Sodom and Gomorrah and became a pillar of salt. It was a reminder and warning of God's plans for us when we look back. Lot's wife wanted to return to the life she had lived in Sodom and Gomorrah, the life from which God was freeing her. It may have seemed like they were leaving someplace so comfortable, but God wanted them rescued from the impending doom of what was already dead. Likewise, we of faith are not to glance longingly back at our old lives. God has freed us from the slavery of our old life be-

DOORWAYS to Greater Faith

fore faith, freed us from the sins of self, pride, and from basking in the imagined "fun" and "comfort" of living in and by the world's rules. This is certain death, and God wants us to choose life.

To list all the facets of faith would be a never-ending task. The depths and heights and wonders of the working of faith — the facets of faith, gives us a glimpse into the endless adventure we can live in this day realizing that God's kingdom of eternal life and power are presently within us. Let us remember Lot's wife and increasingly move into our new life leaving the old behind us. Let us find ourselves fascinated by the wonder of the facets of faith, being eager to learn and exercise them. ✝

CHAPTER 11

EXAMPLES OF FAITH AT WORK
Acts 3:1–16

In Acts 3:1-16, we see Peter and John using what they had learned in Jesus' Faith-Forming School. They had come down from the mountaintop in awe and wonder of Jesus' ascension, and were experiencing a loss and gain as Jesus made wonderful promises of the gift of the Holy Spirit.

Peter and John were going to the temple to pray at three o'clock in the afternoon. As they arrived a forty-year-old man, who had never walked, began asking them for alms. Peter and John *looked intently* at him. The same word is used in Acts 1:10 when the disciples *looked intently* into the sky as the resurrected Savior was lifted up into heaven. Faith was beginning its work in this new life in Peter and John and in those whom they would touch with the power of God that was now within them. It was a continuing adventure into the wonder of the Kingdom of God.

Peter and John were listening for the will of God concerning this man's physical condition. They planned to do God's will, not their own. They were fully aware of Jesus' authority as they had just watched Him ascend to heaven and knew they had been given the task to continue His work. They were fully submitted to this task set before them. Peter and John were not intimidated by this man's problem of being lame from birth. They had the heart of Jesus as they saw this man's problem. All surrendered Christians have experienced knowing God's will about events in their lives. It is normal in a life of faith to have the gift of knowledge. Peter and John were moving in this gift, this facet of faith. They were bold. They remembered how Jesus' power had been present with them. They knew all things were possible with God through the power and authority Jesus had given them.

> *In Peter and John, we begin to see that, in the various ministries we perform, our attention should be focused on both Jesus' heart and the need to which we are ministering.*

They saw the need of the man and were looking for the will of the Lord concerning his need or were waiting for Jesus to say, "*Go for it.*" They submitted to God and would not act on their own initiative. They belonged to God in the same way that they saw Jesus belonged to the Father. They were His bond slaves, willing to let God use their time and energy any way He wanted.

You who belong to God are to act the way Jesus acted with the Father. Jesus often went apart from His followers in order to fellowship with the Father and to get His instructions for His next work. I believe that too often we who follow Him get

11: EXAMPLES OF FAITH AT WORK

swayed by our sympathetic feelings when we pray for the needs of others. Sympathy causes us to pray in such a way that we dip back into our ways before we met Jesus. It causes us to pray out of human sympathy rather than pray the will of God. In these cases, our tactics are often to try to manipulate Him — be it intentional or unintentional. We pray in self-centered ways and for self-centered purposes when our focus in life should really be to imitate Jesus Christ. This is one reason Jesus told us to follow Him by taking up our cross daily. Remember we discussed this before. To take up our cross puts our self-centered ways to death so that Jesus can continue His work using our bodies that we gave to Him.

Peter and John were inquiring intently for God's will concerning the lame man. We ask, "Doesn't God want everyone healed?" Yes, but God has His timing and reasons for situations in each life. There are crises and various other problems that have to happen before we can respond. Remember, He healed only one man among the multitude of the sick, blind, lame, and withered at the well at Bethesda (John 5:2–8). God has His holy and righteous purposes in everything He does. One main purpose He works on in our lives is the opening of that access door of faith. Some need dire circumstances before they are willing to receive the gift of faith or of healing. Others are never willing to receive the gift. All committed Christians will experience trials so that God can test our responses. These tests are usually allowed by God and aimed toward our trouble areas. This gives us opportunity to press further into God's plan for us.

> *One main purpose He works on in our lives is the opening of that access door of faith.*

Peter and John were exercising what they knew Jesus could do through them by their faith. They knew this lame man would be healed, and that it was time to move beyond the ordinary ways of life. They were fully aware and empowered by the knowledge that in the Name of Jesus they could do the impossible. They remembered what Jesus had taught to strengthen their faith, and when they spoke to the lame beggar, expectation blossomed in him as well as in Peter and John.

Peter said, "*I do not possess silver and gold, but what I do have I give to you: In the name of Jesus Christ the Nazarene, walk!*" They transferred their assurance and boldness to the lame man when Peter took hold of his right hand and raised him up. More precisely, the word "*raised*" also means "*awakened*" as in awakening him to faith and health. Paul tells us that it is time for us to awaken from our sleep (See Romans 13:11). God is here, active and involved in our lives.

The lame man got up, leaped and walked around praising God. Yes, he had seen faith and thereby received it. As the people saw the result of faith in the men, they were filled with wonder and amazement. If you remember, we mentioned this once before—God tells us miracles are for those who do not believe, not for those who do, in order that they might see the power of God and believe. Some people will not believe apart from seeing God work in this way. God uses such acts of faith also to strengthen our faith and bring us to a higher place in glory. We grow from glory to glory in Christ Jesus until the glorious day when we will see His beautiful face. Acts 3:7 says the lame man's ankles were strengthened. *Strengthened* is our Greek word for *stereo* that in music refers to sound that sur-

11: EXAMPLES OF FAITH AT WORK

rounds and is firm and strong, where one can hear all the instruments individually. It is amazing how God's word rounds things out for us so beautifully and concisely.

Prior to healing, this lame man had to be carried. He couldn't even stumble along on stiff legs. Apparently, his feet were flopping, as if his leg bones had never fused to his feet properly. When he attempted to stand, he would look down and see both feet turning out to the side causing his legs to give way, having no foundation. His healing happened instantly. What we see is faith at work, Jesus' healing work manifested through faith. Peter and John surely were inquiring of Jesus throughout the duration of this event. Many times, you will find Jesus telling you what to do before you even ask.

Peter and John suddenly were involved in a joyful celebration. When the man who had been lame wasn't leaping and walking and praising God and trying out his new legs by perhaps doing a dance step or two, he was joyfully embracing Peter and John. The excitement must have been electrifying. Faith, once alive, awakens excitement!

It is time for the Church, and that is us, to enter into the excitement of faith. God enters into our celebrations! He created us in His likeness, so He has emotions as well as we do. You remember that Jesus wept! Jesus shared in joy and felt hunger and pain. God feels these things. He is the epitome of the greatest emotion we experience, which is love! What was the Father doing as Peter and John let Jesus heal this blind beggar through them? Why, He was "*Zephaniahing*" it. Watch, Zephaniah 3:17 says, "*The Lord your God is in your midst, a victorious warrior. He will exult over you with joy, He will be quiet in His love,*

He will rejoice over you with shouts of joy." Read that verse again. The reality in this verse is astonishing. God is the victorious warrior exulting over the healed lame man. To *"exult"* is to be *spontaneously cheerful*. It means showing out an internal joy that exceeds the limits of propriety. It means to exhibit exceeding pleasure and cheerfulness. It is the kind of joy that is exhibited with dancing, singing, clapping, screaming and jumping about with laughter! Being *"quiet in His love"* is a beautiful depiction of how God loves us so gently — so deeply — so truly and genuinely that His love causes all of the lame man's sins (and ours) to be forgiven. His sins were forgiven so that no harsh judgment is ever spoken over him. You have this kind of Father in God! You can know this kind of love! This truth blows the concepts of a cold-hearted, distant and uncaring God sky high. He is absolutely approachable — desirous that we should come to Him, open, broken and completely. Your past sins don't surprise the all knowing, all seeing God! He sings over you. He heals you. He forgives you. He dances with you. He celebrates over you. He is taking an active part in your life, and all He wants is your surrender to allow Him to be your God. Don't you just want to know more about Him?✝

Study Questions:

1. Do you believe the same kind of faith is still at work today as the Word says God is the same today as He was yesterday, and will be the same tomorrow?

11: EXAMPLES OF FAITH AT WORK

2. How important is it to pay attention to what Jesus wants you to do when you minister to the needs of others? Do you pray before you minister in His name?
3. Describe a time when you knew God was going to answer your prayer before you even prayed.
4. Describe a time when you knew, while you were praying, that He wasn't going to answer your prayer.
5. Now, what are you going to do since you have a picture of what God revealed He is like in Zephaniah 3:17? How does that change how you view God?

CHAPTER 12

GOD HONORS OUR FAITH
Hebrews 11

It is interesting that Adam and Eve are not mentioned as part of the Hall of Faith membership listed in Hebrews 11. This list includes the saints of old who have gained God's approval. This does not mean Adam and Eve did not have God's approval. Thomas is not listed either because he, too, had his doubts satisfied by seeing. Adam and Eve had no reason to exercise faith because they spoke to God face-to-face, day-by-day. Faith is the assurance of things hoped for, but also those things which are yet *unseen*. Having already seen God and had fellowship with Him, Adam and Eve are not in the list among those who needed to exhibit faith in the unseen. Thomas had his doubt answered by touching and seeing Jesus' wounds. There is an element of trust in our unseen God that these members of the Hall of Faith held onto, hoping against all hope in what God had told, showed or led them to do and be-

12: GOD HONORS OUR FAITH

lieve. Faith asks the believer to have unwavering trust in Him — without ever seeing Him, still to believe. It was by faith that the men of old gained God's approval, gained God's honor (Hebrews 11:2). We see the phrase *"by faith"* eighteen times in Hebrews 11. The names of those men and women who were seed-planters of faith in those generations are mentioned for our benefit. Still, there were countless unnamed others who were also mentioned in Hebrews 11:32-38 who, through their faith, did marvelous works in the power of an unseen God. Many of them suffered various afflictions, including torture and death. Again, many of God's chosen people, today, are suffering affliction and torture as well. They were and are all men and women approved and honored by God.

We see in verse four that, those in Hebrews 11 are dead. Still, their faithful actions speak to us today. Their response to God and the resulting grace of God's work through their lives instructs and speaks to us. The brave people in the Hall of Faith serve as foundational examples for those who are enduring the same things today. The *"by faith"* response to the truth of God in their lives still has an active purpose in our lives as we read of them and their experiences. When we live out a similar faith, we, too, serve as examples for this generation as well as to future generations that follow in our footsteps. Each of us has this purpose and this potential to be a part of God's eternal plan. As we live out what God calls us to do, our acts of faith are honored by God and by men.

Jesus said, *"...if anyone serves Me, the Father will honor him"* (John 12:26b). This facet of faith reminds me of the wonder of God's word in Malachi 3:16. *"Then those who feared the*

Lord spoke to one another, and the Lord gave attention and heard it, and a book of remembrance was written before Him for those who fear the Lord and who esteem His name." God has His own Heavenly Memory Album where He keeps a record of the things we say to each other that honors Him. When we speak our praise reports, God records those reports in the same way we memorialize our own lifetime events in our own memory albums of the things that honor our earthly families. Isn't the thought of this amazing? Yes, God is our Father and He loves us that much! I have a vision in my mind of how God, hearing the wonderful things we say about Him to others, elbows the angels with Him and says, *"Record that in the Book of Remembrance. I want to remember what Bill, Liz, Joe, Mary, and put your name here, just said about Me."* God's honoring of us begins on the day we exhibit faith in our salvation. We hear and believe that there is a grand party in Heaven whenever a new child is born into the Kingdom of God. Luke 15:10 says, *"... there is joy in the presence of the angels of God over one sinner who repents."* The honoring continues as He gives us fellowship with Him. He has promised to never leave or forsake us from this point of our decision process in life on into our eternal life with Him.

One day, as Jesus spoke to His followers, He said, *"I have other sheep* (that's you), *which are not of this fold* (those standing there with Him); *I must bring them also, and they will hear My voice"* (John 10:16 — in parentheses mine). He honors us by sending the Spirit to guide and guard us day-by-day.

> God honors our faith in many ways. One special way He honors us is by recording the good we say about Him in His own Book of Remembrance.

12: GOD HONORS OUR FAITH

You would think there would be no greater honor than being granted God's fellowship and voice. However, there is more. For instance, John 1:12 says we are given the right to become God's children. The word "right," *exousia*, as mentioned before, means that nothing in the whole visible and invisible creation has the power to hinder us from becoming God's children. We need never fear being overwhelmed when we trust in Jesus Christ our Lord. We are His children.

When we trust Him, Ephesians 2:5-7 says God made us alive together with Christ. That is, just as Jesus experienced a resurrected life, we likewise are given that same grace. We are presently alive together with Christ and are raised up and seated with God in Christ Jesus. Now, humbly let this truth work into your awareness. Right now, you are seated with God at His right hand. This is a present and wonderful fact! How can this be? We don't know exactly. It is something spiritual and beyond us.

These wonders open us to the surpassing riches of God's grace in our present lives. Ephesians 2:7 reads, *"So that in the ages to come, He might show the surpassing riches of His grace in kindness toward us in Christ Jesus."* Let's remember that verse the next time we come before the Lord with any request. God honors our faith now and right on into eternity.

Through these wonders, God begins a work in us that He calls, *"His workmanship."* He is continually transforming us into new people. We enter into this understanding of our newness as far as our own minds can comprehend. This is why God tells us to ask for wisdom. However, we know that a battle is going on in our minds as Satan tries to deceive us, hoping that

DOORWAYS to Greater Faith

we will have difficulty accepting who we are in Christ. God's voice is easy to recognize for those of us who have surrendered to Jesus as our Great Shepherd. Jesus said that His sheep hear His voice. We are to do those urgings in our mind that are in agreement with God's Word, not those urgings that contradict what God has said or those urgings that feed our fleshly appetites. He leads us into truth. We are His workmanship.

We honor Him by obeying Him, in spite of what we see, think or feel. He honors us, as we commit ourselves to Him, by allowing us to move deeper and deeper into His call for our lives. His call includes us becoming increasingly like Jesus Christ.

We are greatly honored as God works the transformation of Christ's likeness in us. He honors us by allowing us to move deeper and still deeper into His call for us to advance into our full potential in serving Him. Once we were dead to our trespasses and sins, God honors us by giving us a way out of that life and into God's new life through Jesus Christ. We experience that life increasingly by obeying His leading in this new life He is working in us.

> *Each of us possesses power to prevail over every crisis, every situation, and every circumstance in our life.*

Paul said, *"For if by the transgressions of one* (Adam), *death reigned through the one, much more those who receive the abundance of grace and of the gift of righteousness will reign in life through the One, Jesus Christ"* (Romans 5:17 in parentheses mine). Did He say, *"Reign in life?"* Yes. An unending library of books could be written concerning everything that *reigning in life* entails. The apostle John, speaking of further wonders that Christ did for

12: GOD HONORS OUR FAITH

us, said, *"There are also many other things which Christ did, which, if they were written in detail, I suppose that even the world itself would not contain the books that would be written"* (John 21:25). Such books would speak further concerning our reigning in life. We have everything written that we need in the Bible. Still, there is much to be learned and understood concerning everything about what we already have. Here, as we discuss *reigning in life*, there is only one way to speak inclusively of this position of honor we maintain while being toughened up as life tends to threaten this position.

Simply put, each of us possesses power to prevail over every crisis, every situation, and every circumstance in our lives by turning to Jesus Christ in that circumstance. We can reign over every mountain-like situation we face and over every anxiety. Remember how Jesus repeated over and over that we should not fear, nor be anxious? Our reign in this new life is to be over all the situations this world and Satan cause us to face, and there are and will be many. In Revelation 5:10 (KJV), we read of the four beasts and twenty elders singing a new song that ends: *"And hast made us unto our God kings and priests: and we shall reign on the earth."* Can you hear it? We reign right now as we boldly refuse to allow worldly problems, pleasures and temptations to distress, distract or sway us.

God still honors faith today. The honorees listed in our Hall of Faith in Hebrews eleven did not exhaust the many ways that God honors our faith. For instance, we are honored every time God answers our prayers. Every time we are thankful and every time we praise Him, there is an honor that is given because of our activity of praising and thanking God. In addition to honoring God, our exercised faith is how we grow further into our potential. As we honor God, He honors us, and in perfect love, He continues to honor us.†

Study Questions:

1. What are the marks of God's approval and honoring in your life?
2. How can you make the "by faith" phrase spoken of in the Bible more meaningful in your living and witnessing?
3. How does it impress you that God has so worked in your life that you can reign in your circumstances?
4. What was your experience when you accepted Jesus Christ as your Savior?
5. In what other ways has God honored you? Have you praised Him, as those in the Hall of Faith did, even when many of them did not see the fulfillment of God's promises in their lifetime?

CHAPTER 13

THE RISK FACTOR IN FAITH
Luke 1:26-38; Matthew 4:1-11

Faith expressed in one's life carries a risk factor along with it. The nature of faith requires risk because faith involves us stepping forward into the unknown. We are told that faith is the conviction of things not seen. By faith, we understand God created everything that we see out of things that are invisible (Hebrews 11:1,3). Faith, then, requires our trusting God for that which we do not see. It demands that we put aside our trust in our fleshly senses and emotions — those things which we see, touch and feel. When the Israelites were told to step into the raging Jordan River, they believed God that they could cross it and go into the land God had promised them. Once they took the first step, the river parted, but they had to take the first step. We are to trust God regardless of what we see around us. Peter walked on the water the same way. We have first steps to take also, and they come more often than we realize. I know that God would have us learn to be more sensitive. Looking into the facet of faith that reveals risk, think about the risk Mary took in giving birth to Jesus. This little teenage girl had to deal with facing the extraordinary. How could she have a baby? She was a virgin. Gabriel answered her question: The baby would be conceived by the power of God.

Here are some risks Mary faced: What would her betrothed, Joseph, think? Would he understand? We are told Joseph planned to divorce her quietly so as not to disgrace her. God had to send an angel to Joseph to explain the circumstances of her pregnancy (Matthew 1:19-21). God takes care of us when we face risks in our obedience. There were even more risks. What would her family think, her friends, the people in her village? Mary and Joseph both knew the risk of the gossip. Those in the neighborhood surely would not understand. For Mary to fulfill God's calling in her life, her faith had to surpass all of her senses. She risked her entire life to follow God's will and be the mother of our Savior. We can surely learn by her example of unwavering faith! We must follow the example of Mary and Joseph and obey God regardless of the risk. To obey God we must not be concerned about what others say or think.

Liz and I have a friend who is determined to obey God regardless of the risk. She is finding opposition in surprising places. She says it is a continuing struggle. As her choice is to follow Jesus, it threatens those who are not equally determined. When you follow God faithfully, you enter into risky situations and even risk the loss of some relationships.

13: THE RISK FACTOR IN FAITH

Perhaps it would benefit us if we would think of the faith it took our Lord Jesus to become a man. He laid aside His privileges as God in order to experience every temptation, trial and risk that we face. We are told He was made like us in all things, so He could be a merciful and faithful High Priest to us in our weaknesses and sins. See Hebrews 2:17.

That is how He understands the temptations and situations and risks we face. He faced them as well. Therefore, He knows how to deliver us in the midst of our trials. Notice that in the Bible, we are continually turned to Jesus, as our *way* in all things! You remember how Jesus separated Himself for times of solitude with God to pray for direction and to worship the Father? We need to do the same. We need time with God to regenerate our faith and discover His will for us, just as Jesus did.

Though we will study the temptation of Jesus in chapter 15 in more detail, we will consider it here in order to study the risk factor in faith. As Satan began his attack on Jesus, he challenged, *"If You are the Son of God, make some bread out of these stones."* Here Jesus faced the risk of putting His needs ahead of God's call and will for His life.

We are tempted the same way. The risks of faith are ever before us. In addition, we have to be alert and wise because we can intercept and negate God's will for us by seeking to meet needs that are more for earthly comforts and get side tracked from our destiny.

The second temptation of Jesus was when Satan says to Him, *"If you are the Son of God, throw yourself off the highest point of the temple. People will see angels swoop down to save you, as the Bible says."* The enticement was to take an easy way to prove who He was and to do it His way rather than God's way. How easy it becomes for us to worry about making something of ourselves. How many times have believers reached for new jobs elsewhere thinking they are "led by God" to do so, when they have not inquired of God at all. There are those few events when God does ask us to walk away from things — but those are worldly things. Abraham's father was a maker of false idols when God asked Abraham to leave his home. God doesn't *usually* take us away from our commitments — especially when we, ourselves, have made that commitment. We cannot walk in faith and then continue to do things our way. We must be sure to follow the voice of God — not our own will or the voice of the enemy. Much to my dismay, this can easily happen to any of us — it even happens with ministers and with other leaders in the church as well.

How surprising it is when people easily think we can hold off our commitment to God for a future time. Jesus spoke of this in Luke 9:57-62. A man came wanting to follow Jesus. Jesus told him, *"Follow Me." "All right,"* the man answered. *"I will come as soon as my father dies, perhaps in a few years."* Jesus answered him and other such offers: *"No one, after putting his hand to the plow and looking back, is fit for the kingdom of God."* The Bible teaches that looking back; waiting for a more appropriate time is one of the greatest determents of God's will in our lives. God expects immediate obedience. Delayed obedience is disobedience.

God went so far as to tell us that obedience is better than sacrifice. Anyone who has sacrificed anything at all for someone else — for God, understands the meaning of sacrifice.

13: THE RISK FACTOR IN FAITH

Jesus sacrificed His life, but God is telling us how important our obedience is to our walk. We will surely miss God if we do not follow Him — when He calls!

In the third temptation, Satan offered to give Jesus what He was actually working toward anyway — all the kingdoms of the world and their glory, if Jesus would worship him (Satan). It was a risk then, and it always will be, to worship anything but Almighty God. The enticement is especially evident as we see Jesus praying before His death in the Garden of Gethsemane. When we think of Jesus there, it seems impossible that Jesus, who knew all things that were coming upon Him (John 18:4), could be deeply grieved to the point of sweating so profusely that His sweat became like drops of blood. (Luke 22:44) He spoke of being deeply distressed and troubled (Matthew 26:37-38 and Mark 14:33-34). Let us remember this the next time we are distressed or troubled. Jesus went through quite a bit of distress and trouble for us, too. He was a real human being, there in the garden, with real human emotions.

He wasn't ever alone, though. The Father was with Him. Peter, James, and John were not there in the Garden of Gethsemane to pray with Jesus. They were along to pray for themselves, that they would not enter into temptation. See Matthew 26:41. Instead of praying, they grew weary and went to sleep. As they slept, Jesus was watching and praying so He would not yield to temptation. How many times have we fell asleep while praying? We run a high risk when we don't watch and pray for God's protection over our family, and friends, and our nation. One wonders if Peter would not have denied Jesus if they had watched and prayed. All of this happened for a reason, if only to show us that we need to be watchful and not grow weary in our warfare against temptation in our own lives. The enemy is on the prowl seeking whom he can kill and destroy. This is no game. We are to be mindful of our enemy.

When Jesus told them to watch and pray, the word "watch" is a command to be continuously attentive and vigilant, to be cautious in one's behavior and in fervent prayer. All the faithful are called to make this a continuous activity in our own lives. We face the same risks in our faith. It is a risk for every Christian when we first decide to give our lives to Jesus by faith. Others will ridicule our new life style. God tells us to have no other gods before Him... that means family, work, projects, thoughts, feelings, self preservation... nothing! I have to say I have often fallen short. Praise God for the saving grace of Jesus.

> *Righteous people are humble enough to let God change how they think, what they do, and where they go.*

Let us remember, we are talking about how risky it is to serve God. A risk factor is always present. Some time ago, I heard a preacher talking about the youth of the Church he served. He spoke of how risky they were in practicing their faith. He said they would go to the local shopping centers to witness, and when they saw someone sick or needy they would go and ask if they could pray for that person. In an environment where teenage peer pressure can be severe and the ramifications of standing out for God can cause even beatings and sometimes worse, these youth were taking a great risk to step out in faith and help others. Asking a stranger if you can help them spiritually, carries risk for any of us! People become

13: THE RISK FACTOR IN FAITH

offended or think you are a nutcase, wanting to stand in the middle of a shopping center and pray! These teens even faced ridicule from those they desired to help, just the same as Jesus. God answered their boldness by healing those for whom they prayed. God answers the faithful and fervent prayers of the righteous. Stepping out in pure and risky faith touches the heart of God. Remember, too, that God counts your faith as righteousness and also, that without faith it is impossible to please God.

I remember going into a restaurant once and sitting with my wife and two children, next to a table with six truck drivers whose language was a bit more colorful than I desired my children to hear. As we waited for our meal and I was cringing at what I was hearing, I began to wonder if I should say a prayer of grace over our meal, as we usually do. When our food arrived, I cranked up my boldness and our family bowed our heads and thanked God for our food. The truck drivers became strangely quiet during our prayer and the language became completely acceptable afterward. Risky faith, in that situation, opened a door of respect. It also changed the way others viewed their own behavior. We can expect God to work on our behalf when we pray in risky places.

I remember when a men's fellowship of our Church met for breakfast at a Cracker Barrel restaurant one morning. There were about eight of us. I asked one to pray. He did, boldly, more loudly than I would have done, more loudly than I thought necessary for our little group. I looked up during the prayer; curious to see what was happening in the room that had grown quiet. To my amazement, every head in the half

DOORWAYS to Greater Faith

filled restaurant was bowed in prayer. One man had a filled fork poised halfway to his mouth as he respectfully prayed. Never allow the enemy to entice us to assume the worst. Do what God says to do and let Him work out the details.

Wonderful things happen when Christians risk being who they are meant to be, children of an Almighty God with a purpose. He is interested in all the details of our lives. To be a man or woman of faith will carry risks because many of those around you are unable to see the invisible as the eyes of faith see. This is why God calls us, *"the light of the world."* I believe God especially watches and blesses all who risk their comfort, reputation and, sometimes, their lives to help others see God through their faith that their action makes visible. ✝

STUDY QUESTIONS:

1. In what ways have you risked your own comfort and reputation to do something God asked you to do?
2. How can you make the "by faith" phrase of the Bible more meaningful in your living and witnessing?
3. What are some things you have discovered in your watching and waiting that you can share with others?
4. Share your insight with examples of risky faith that you have observed in the Bible.
5. What are some risky things you have felt called to do? What is the Lord saying to you about them? Has the enemy tried to entice you to do them his way or your way? How?

13: THE RISK FACTOR IN FAITH

6. Have you ever been called by God, knew it and didn't step out, only to watch someone else do what God asked you to do? Did you learn the lesson to answer the call when God calls? Express this situation with the group as you feel comfortable.

CHAPTER 14

ᚠAITH ᚠS ᚱEVOLUTIONARY
Luke 4:17–19; Acts 17:1–9

In each facet of faith, we see increasingly more deeply into the wonders the Lord offers us presently and also for eternity. In both cases, now and for eternity, Jesus tells us that what He offers is so transforming and wonderful that, if it were a treasure hidden in a field, a person would sell everything he or she possessed to buy that field. See Matthew 13:44. Again, He said what He offers us through faith in Him has such transforming power, it works in the human life like leaven in bread. We are increasingly transformed until everything about us is changed (Matthew 13:33).

What happens through faith in Jesus in every believer is that His life in us changes us, and then He works through us to change the world about us. Paul said the Lord Jesus rescued us from the authority of darkness, and we are transferred into the

14: FAITH IS REVOLUTIONARY

kingdom of God. We belong there now (Colossians 1:13). We are (present tense, as in today, as in right now) rescued out of the devil's hold on us. We quickly see that faith is a revolutionary word. Faith is a mightier relationship with God than we yet realize. The revolutionary part of faith is how God's kingdom breaks into this world's kingdom and rescues us from the worldly system in which we mistakenly think we have to live. We are set free! This is what Paul spoke of at one point. Through faith in Christ, we are transported from this world of darkness and into God's glorious light, love, and grace. Understanding the liberty we are given, we tap into the magnificent power of God, which can happen only by the power of faith! We live above the physical in a new spiritual realm.

In Luke 4:17, Jesus quotes from Isaiah, Chapter 61, speaking this truth about our freedom from oppression, setting the captives of this world free! *"The Spirit of the Lord is upon Me, because He anointed Me to preach the Gospel to the poor. He sent Me to proclaim release to the captives, and recovery of sight to the blind, to set free those who are oppressed, to proclaim the favorable year of the Lord"* (Luke 4:18-19).

Then Jesus says, in verse 21, that this Bible verse has been fulfilled, just now, in your hearing from the One sent to release us. Now, the call our Lord had has become our present responsibility as well. We are the chosen ones called to preach the Gospel to the poor, to proclaim release to the captives, to fulfill that same calling that Jesus had upon His life from the Father. There are other wonders in all this. Have you noticed something hampering your relationships with friends or strangers, with your spouse or children, something holding you back, that you would like to be released from, so you can enter more deeply into your relationship with Jesus and with others? Jesus came to release the captives, to make the chains fall off your wrists and legs and also to remove the shackles from your heart and mind. Like the chains and shackles fell off Peter, and the locked doors of the prison swung open to him in Acts 12, we too, must understand that we are free. If a bird has been caged all of its life, you can open the door to his cage and it will probably not ever venture out. If a bird knows it does not belong in that cage, it will squawk and carry on until you open the door and let the bird out. Let us not be like the caged bird who accepts captivity, but realize that we have been born anew as free creatures in Christ.

As Jesus speaks this to you, understand that these healings and revolutionary transformations come by faith in what the Name of Jesus will do through you today. Jesus cannot fail to accomplish such transformations in each believer. Expect it!

Living by faith is a miraculous work of God in your life as you walk closer and closer following Him, moving on into truth.

"*Now faith is the assurance of things hoped for*" or "*Faith is the substance* (the spiritual building materials) *of things hoped for*" (Hebrews 11:1 in parenthesis mine). God wants us to move on into His promises. Don't let fear of what others think of you keep you in the chains, but love them by teaching them God's truths and allow for their release, too!. You feel stuck because you know you should step out, but fear has stifled the Word God has for you to share. Step out in faith, and watch God work through you. We can

14: FAITH IS REVOLUTIONARY

open the Bible to almost any page and see God working in lives, and these lives are being amazingly changed in glorious ways. We also see this today in the lives of those who move out in bold faith. We may suffer persecution at some point, but the reward of knowing that some have heard and are also freed from the grip of Satan, makes the persecution worth the pain.

Jesus demonstrated what a human life, lived wide open for God, looks like — human life as God designed us to live. Jesus said of His human life practices, *"Truly, truly, I say to you, the Son can do nothing of Himself, unless it is something He sees the Father doing; for whatever the Father does, these things the Son also does in like manner"* (John 5:19). Again He said, *"I do not seek My own will, but the will of Him who sent Me"* (John 5:30). Furthermore, Jesus said He did nothing on His own initiative, but that He spoke the things the Father spoke to Him (John 8:28).

Jesus demonstrated a revolutionary way of living and praying that many Christians have not understood, as of yet, how to enter. This way of living must be for God's purposes, not ours. We are to pray with more than our minds. We pray in a way where we begin by focusing on God. We don't premeditate our prayers or rehearse them. We focus on God, then pray the thoughts He puts in our minds.

Everything about faith revolutionizes us because we are transferred into the kingdom of God and a life far above what we could have ever expected in our human way of thinking. God has plans for us, and we will keep on changing since the kingdom is God's spiritual leaven in us. As we grow, we are changing into Christ's likeness as we allow the Spirit to transform us. It is a joyful, amazing, peaceful and exciting journey.

DOORWAYS to Greater Faith

As we enter more and more fully, we will understand that it is worth everything we possess in this world, even our lives to have found this place. Being under the yoke of the kingdom of darkness, the world lives under a cloud of deception, and if they would pray, their prayers are selfish prayers. Note in Acts 4 that Peter and John were on trial for healing a lame man and preaching about Jesus' resurrection from the dead. They were on trial for healing someone? Can you imagine?

As Peter and John stood accused, they caused amazement in the Sanhedrin court. Acts 4:13 is a good example of the revolutionary activity of faith in a Christian's life. Paul and John were uneducated and untrained, and yet were so confident, so free from the world's customs, so bold in their speaking, and so assured in what they were saying that their judges recognized them as having been with Jesus. We often forget that John was uneducated as well as the other writers of our treasured Bible. We call their writings "inspired," for God spoke through them. Some uneducated men of our own day astound the wise as they live and breathe, teach and exercise God's Word to this dying world! Do not ever think that you are not able. With God all things are possible! Greater is He who is in you than He who is in the world.

> *Each believer, through their faith, and as Jesus purposes, is to open every door that presently holds us in a prison away from present kingdom life.*

Consider the world's shout and angry accusations in Acts 17:1-9. Some Jews and Greeks and a number of leading women had responded to Paul's teachings about Jesus. The Jews became jealous and violently shouted, *"These that have turned the*

14: FAITH IS REVOLUTIONARY

world upside down are come hither also" (Acts 17:6 KJV). Really, the world is so deceived that it believes we, as Christians, are trying to cause problems. This world was turned upside down when Satan tempted Adam and Eve and they fell into sin. The world we were born into as babies is upside down. Faith in Jesus Christ actually turns the world back right side up, and the world complains when it happens around them because change usually makes people uncomfortable. People of the world who want to stay there don't want anyone messing around with their comfort zone. Unknown to them, and what Jesus is trying to show them, is that the only way to true peace is living like Jesus and letting Him open their prison door to find life. Contrary to what the world thinks, we don't live for today, but for the hope of glory in our eternal life. If we step out in revolutionary faith, we can show them the way out of the darkness and into the light. They will have eternal life, just like us — but it will be an eternal life of death and separation from God. We must continue to do God's will and step out in the extraordinary belief that God will do all that He has promised in the Bible for you and those you touch. Faith *is* revolutionary. It changes us and the world around us and brings those who need Jesus to a realization of the change they, too, need!✝

> *We ourselves are receiving the call to live by faith - right now!*

STUDY QUESTIONS:

1. What does it mean to you when someone speaks of a revolution of your life?

DOORWAYS to Greater Faith

2. Has faith permeated your life so that you can sense God's presence with you and His pleasure over you? Do you understand the power and work of the Spirit within you?
3. What revolution or change has occurred in your thoughts that have released you from your personal prisons? Have you helped others escape the same prisons by your testimony to them?
4. Can you be specific about changes in you that separate you from the world's ways and teachings?
5. What do you think makes the world so uncomfortable about change? When they see your revolutionary faith, what is their response?

CHAPTER 15

The Mind of Faith
Matthew 4:1-11

As I researched the Bible about the mind of faith, I was surprised at the different mind-types that are mentioned. For instance, the Bible speaks of the reprobate mind, the carnal mind, the vain mind, and an alienated mind. It also speaks of humble minds, of willing and faithful minds and of other mind-types.

Since faith is the assurance of things for which we hope, having a mind of faith gives the Christian a peaceful mind. Such minds are positive and assured because God has touched them in such a way that they are renewed.

Paul tells us to *"be renewed in the spirit of your minds"* (Ephesians 4:23). With those words, he wonderfully releases us from the impossible task of fixing our own minds because *"to be renewed'* is written purposefully in a passive form, meaning God is the One who renews our minds. This also means that we are to fix our eyes on Jesus Christ and, in obedience, surrender to this renewing process. He has given, and continues to give us, everything we need in order to be like Him. His instruction concerning our part in this is found where God says we are to study the Bible to show ourselves approved, accurately handling the Word of truth (II Timothy 2:15). He has done the work and continues the work in you! This renewal is a continual process. That is, God is continually renewing our minds or hearts as we continually study His Word in the Bible. What is happening to us in this area is not yet a done deal, and it won't be "done" as long as we live. We feel a struggle in this area of truth. Something is struggling against what God is doing in us. It is the enemy, who continually tries to deceive us and bankrupt our mind. It is Satan who tries to deceive and twist our minds in His temptation the same as he did with Jesus.

Do not be fearful about this battle in your mind. It is a normal spiritual activity that goes on in every one of us while we are here on this earth. It is good to remember that we are never alone in such battles. Jesus put us on guard when He urged us to watch our words and emotions, and to guard our minds. As we resist the devil in his activity here, God promises that the enemy will flee from us.

What we are speaking of is not something otherworldly. It goes on at every opportune moment in your life, as it did with Jesus. We read of this in Luke 4:13, which says the devil left Jesus, until an opportune time. Opportune moments for the enemy would be in times of stress or loss, times of weakness or

15: THE MIND OF FAITH

sickness, when we endure bad news, when we are out of fellowship and/or when we don't obey the Lord. We are therefore to be deliberate in putting on our new self that is the likeness of God. Think about it and choose to be like Jesus in these life moments when you are struggling. As we are renewed in our mind and put on the new self (Ephesians 4:23-24), we take part in reaching to the desired result. You are to choose to be personally involved in taking part in this battle for your mind and your new self in Christ.

We are to defend the new mind that God has given us. This new mind refers to one that is literally a new creation. Watch this battle taking place in the mind of Jesus and see how it is won. In Matthew 4:1-11, Jesus had just finished fasting for forty days and forty nights. At the end of such a fast, a person's hunger becomes overwhelming, signaling starvation is near. In a normal, human state of existence, one must start eating as this is the means to physical survival.

This is an opportune moment of weakness where Satan attacks. He steps in to take advantage of Jesus' human condition. Think of this in the same way that temptation comes to us. Remember that for something to be a temptation, it must be what one really wants or senses is a physical need. It must appeal to our deepest desire. This is the definition of temptation.

At one time, I thought Satan appeared to Jesus in a physical manifestation. Now, I have come to realize the temptation came to Jesus the same way it comes to us. The enemy (Satan) attacks in our minds and in our thoughts. Hebrews 4:15 tells us that Jesus, "*has been tempted in all things as we are, yet without sin.*" Jesus faced the same battles in His mind that you and I face in ours. Friend, you are never alone, and you never have to confront your enemy alone. This is a great comfort to us.

The first temptation Jesus faced was Satan's attempt to deceive Jesus, to make Him doubt that He is God's Son. This should not surprise us, even though at Jesus' baptism a few days before, God had announced, *"This is My beloved Son, in whom I am well-pleased"* (Matthew 3:17). Jesus heard the Father call Him His, *"Son."* Still, Satan attempted to cause Jesus, as a man, to doubt God's word. As the opportunity of temptation began, Satan, twisting God's words to his advantage in each temptation, challenged: *"If You are the Son of God, command that these stones become bread"* (Matthew 4:3). Jesus' mind and His faith were attacked and were on trial here. If Jesus had doubted for a moment, that He is God's Son, God would have failed in bringing salvation into the world. He would not be God. I believe all creation would have dissolved into nothing because all the purposes of our Creator God in His creation would have been negated.

You and I are familiar with this type of temptation as this attack on our minds is something of which we have been subject. God said, *"For you are all sons of God through faith in Christ Jesus"* (Galatians 3:26). You are God's son, God's daughter, His child. Remember, we just said Jesus was facing this challenge to doubt. Have you ever doubted that you are God's child? Do you see this? Jesus faced the same temptation. I have heard many say, *"Well, I hope I am His child."* There is an element of doubt in such a statement! God also said: The one who doubts (in his mind) *"ought not to expect that he will receive anything from the Lord"* (James 1:7). For God to confront our doubt in us in

15: THE MIND OF FAITH

this fashion is not an attack on us, but it is meant to let us know that we are accountable for how we believe and where we keep our own focus. It is also a call to waste no time in getting into a dedicated and daily personal relationship with God, through faith in Jesus Christ. Our relationship with God should be such a relationship that our mind never wavers from a full commitment to Jesus Christ and the promises in God's Word. This is not a difficult task; children can do it. Guess what? You can, too! It is simply a commitment of your will. Just as Jesus was tempted to doubt God's Word in His mind, we are often faced with this same mental attack. With a choice to have faith, you can defeat doubt.

The second temptation emphasizes the doubt: Satan reverts to a new attack, saying to Jesus, "*If you are the Son of God, throw yourself off the highest point of the temple...Doesn't the Bible say that the angels...will bear You up...and keep you from stumbling?*" (Paraphrase from Matthew 4:6) Satan tried to persuade Jesus that the people would be so impressed to see the angels swoop down and come to Jesus' rescue. He implied that this act would cause them to believe in Jesus when they saw this wondrous sight, and then, the people would worship Him. Again the temptation was for Jesus to doubt His identity and His destiny — God's purpose for Him. Perhaps this might have had a temporary allure for the people, but this was not God's plan and not God's way of bringing salvation to the world. Jesus knew this and, once again, chose God's plan versus the wiles of the enemy. This attack mirrors what the en-

> *Be aware of the tactics of your enemy! The Holy Spirit promises to lead us into all truth.*

emy tries to do to believers who set out to do God's will. When they get tired, when they've waited so long for God to bring about His promises, the enemy comes in at the time of weakness and tries to persuade us to do things a quick way — our way and not God's way. It is so easy for Christians to accept things as true that are not Biblical truths. We must be careful to keep in constant prayer, know we hear God's voice and do His will alone. The battle for the mind rages on and so many yield. God tells us in His Word that we are to *"humble yourself under the mighty hand of God, that He may exalt you at the proper time"* (1 Peter 5:6). All we need to do is humble ourselves. We don't even need to hold ourselves up, but just wait on God. There is nothing better than to be in the midst of God's will.

The third temptation occurs after Satan shows Jesus all the kingdoms of the world and their glory. Satan then says to Him, *"All these things I will give You, if You fall down and worship me"* (Matthew 4:9). Satan wanted to be put ahead of God and to be worshiped. He still does. If Jesus had done this, it would have been God bowing down and worshipping Satan. How upside down *that* would have been! Jesus had the Father first in His mind, which is also His heart. Now, we *are* children of God. We are to have our hearts fixed in the same way as Jesus — on God. The heart is that place in mankind that houses our will, our desire, our attention, our thinking. It is also considered our mind — the completeness of who we are, our full consciousness of being.

God (the Father, the Son, and the Holy Spirit) are to be our focus, that for which our minds hunger and yearn. That yearn-

15: THE MIND OF FAITH

ing, in the Bible, is compared to a man leaving his father and mother and being joined to his wife (Ephesians 5:31). Remember those times men, ladies? I remember the yearning. I remember working at my job while my mind, my heart yearned for my wife; I thought of her. I could not get her off my mind. I did not want to get her off my mind. I still think of her every moment. I still love her and want her and hold her in my mind. I have even prayed, asking God to give me new ways to express my love to her. *That* is how we are to hold God in our minds and hearts, as well. How can a believer ever let his or her mind be turned away from God and His desires for us? The answer is that a truly surrendered believer, committed to God, cannot.

We must set our minds like a flint to be God's people. We are new creatures in Christ, who have His mind forming in us. Philippians 2:5 (KJV) reads, *"Let this mind be in you, which was also in Christ Jesus."* ☦

Study Questions:

1. How do you protect yourself or defend your mind when opportune moments arise for the enemy's attacks?
2. Can you tell the difference between Satan's words and God's words? Notice that Satan attacks and condemns and seeks to hurt you and deny the Bible in your thoughts. God encourages and loves; warns and points you to His Word and comfort. The Holy Spirit leads as He communicates to us by peace.

3. In what weak areas do you feel Satan attacks your mind? What are some Biblical passages that you can use to stop him and cause him to flee?
4. Is your mind set to be God's man; God's woman? What do you do to encourage such a mind set? In what ways do you sense the transformation of your heart and mind?

CHAPTER 16

ꝔAITH ꟽOVES ꝔORWARD
John 1:12; Mark 8:34–35

Imagine faith like a precious, perfectly cut diamond with many sides, each revealing its clarity. Each facet of a diamond reveals new colors and dynamics of the diamond, lending to its beauty. As we look into each facet, we also see remarkable clarity for each facet is a face of the diamond revealing a different side to the character of the diamond. By studying each of the different facets of faith, we discover a delightful way of seeing the value of faith with greater clarity. We expectantly tilt and turn the diamond of faith to catch further glimpses as we seek to know it more completely.

We reiterate for the sake of our subject that faith is the assurance of things for which we hope. What we hope for is the full expression of the Gospel in our lives. We read of one aspect of that expression in John 1:12: *"But as many as received*

Him, to them He gave the right to become children of God, even to those who believe in His name." Once we receive Jesus Christ as our Savior, we become a child of God... a son or daughter of God, adopted into the family with all the benefits and glory becoming our own inheritance. At the moment of our adoption (our moment of realizing who Jesus is and what He came here to do for us), each of us is given what we need to live a life of imitating Jesus. He now is our big brother. Just as we see younger siblings imitating their older siblings, we can choose to do the same. God gives us that right to choose. Jesus came here to earth to be our example, but we must choose to live that life. Life is about choices! This is a good point to remember and pass on to your family.

There is great authority in the *right* to make this choice, because the Greek word for *right, exousia,* denies the presence of any hindrance. Faith in Jesus opens the door for us to choose life actions as God's children and nothing can actually hinder us in such choices. God does not even interfere with our free will to choose. Just like Jesus faced temptations to choose other actions, we will also face temptations aimed at preventing us from making the correct choices. As Jesus was tempted, we will be tempted to deny God's will for our lives, tempted to worship something else beside God and tempted not to believe we are children of God. We are continually tempted not to follow Jesus.

Now as His children we are to move forward in this kind of faith. Faith is the assurance, the substance, a spiritual material reality of the things for which we hope in the Gospel (Hebrews 11:1). Things like *forgiven sin* and the *resulting peace and joy* and

16: FAITH MOVES FORWARD

freshness of life are evidences of a spiritual material in us. These are material witnesses of the hope in us that we are the sons and daughters of God! Lest we forget, in the New Testament *hope* means *"confident expectation."* We can walk in the full assurance and confidence, beyond all doubt, that we indeed are God's sons and daughters. We can walk this out in faith.

As we look deeper into the facet of faith that is moving us forward, we hear Jesus calling over, and over: *"Follow Me."* When Jesus calls us, He means for us to walk in His footsteps, to live as He lived. This is the path on which God calls us to move onward. It is the good news of the Gospel. We disciples of Christ are, by faith, to move after Him as His first disciples moved. Mark 8:34,35 reads, *"And He summoned the crowd with His disciples, and said to them, 'If anyone wishes to come after Me, he must deny himself, and take up his cross and follow Me. For whoever wishes to save his life will lose it, but whoever loses his life for My sake and the gospel's will save it.'"*

All believers, not just the disciples, are called to follow Jesus. Please notice that in losing our present self-centered life, which we have learned is, *"taking up our cross,"* we walk with a new life focus. Therefore, we deliberately walk into this new life we have chosen. Faith moves us forward from where we were to where God now calls us.

In chapter fourteen, we discussed the facet of faith that is revolutionary, that angle of the diamond of faith that reveals the change in our hearts and minds. Here we see the change occurring as a progression. Faith does always move us forward. There really is no way to walk in faith and not move forward. We are called to follow, to follow Him which is a forward progression in life-changing ways as we become more like Christ on a continual basis. As we walk with Jesus Christ, following His ways, we move close to Him.

The side distractions that bother us are the same as those that tempted Jesus. Every temptation was meant to prevent Jesus from fulfilling what the Father sent Him to do. They were meant to stall His forward movement. The goal of Satan was that Jesus would worship him or that He would depend upon Himself instead of doing the will of the Father. Likewise, we are tempted to follow worldly leaders, popular teachers, even misguided ministers and, sadly, even our own foolish plans. It seems like the easier route, at times, to take our eyes off Jesus Christ and the purpose that God has for our lives. What God asks us to do is not going to be easy. Even when it would have been easier for Jesus to do things the way Satan suggested, Jesus knew God's way was the only way for Him. The reward for doing God's will is eternal. At the point where we get our eyes off Jesus, all forward momentum in our faith stops. We are to have one focus only and that is to have the mind of Christ. Jesus said He came to preach to the poor, to release the captives, to open our physical and spiritual eyes, and to set free those whose lives are crushed, bruised or oppressed. Christ has set us free (Galatians 5:1). When we walk in faith, we rise above oppression. Freedom means to be unrestricted by, or to be freed from the authority of sin; freed into all the gospel privileges in order

Faith includes your willingness to leave behind the things you have learned concerning the world's ways, and when God speaks, to move forward into the new wisdom He reveals to you.

16: FAITH MOVES FORWARD

to make us willing slaves of God (I Peter 2:16). In this, Jesus frees us from those things that hinder our faith, that hold us in a place of hurt and keep us living stagnant lives. By faith, we confidently stretch toward things hoped for that move us forward from where we are now. Faith keeps us following and reaching after Jesus Christ.

We are moving forward into a new culture and into a new environment of learning and living. We have access into something glorious: God's continual presence. We have deliberately chosen a new way of life that has set us apart from the grip of this world as we follow the example of Jesus and live for God. The life of God's kingdom dweller moves a person toward what is more precious than anything we earnestly desire in this world. We know there is a new day and new life eternal. God has a special purpose for us. This is what we believe and what gives us such great fulfillment and freedom. We have liberty to be who God created us to be, and we have faith that God is preserving us for eternity. This world pales in comparison to what God has in store for us here and for eternity. Jesus reminds us of this frequently. Through faith, God is drawing us close to Him and closer to understanding our walk with Him! We do not desire to stand still as faith moves us with that desire to possess our new life. ✝

Study Questions:

1. Can you identify the ways you are moving forward in your faith?
2. What does it mean to you to watch or guard your words and emotions?

3. Have you ever been or are you presently tempted to follow anyone or anything in place of Jesus Christ, including your own plans?
4. In what way has Jesus Christ freed you? Can you point to specific things that hindered you before or imprisoned your mind?
5. How are you using that freedom?

CHAPTER 17

LIVING BY FAITH – PART ONE
Various Bible Verses

What does it mean to live by faith? "By faith," is a phrase we often hear in Christian circles. It is a phrase that describes life in its fullest sense; life as God means for all to experience. However, the phrase sometimes becomes just a fancy religious expression that many of us do not fully understand. Both the Old and the New Testament are full of the wonders worked by God in and through those who lived by faith. By faith, Moses defeated the strongest nation of his time; by faith, Stephen performed wonders and signs; by faith, God is pleased. The Lord still works wonders through those of us who have faith in our generation. Many Christians, although, are hampered by their own misunderstanding and absence of faith. They remain clothed in the things of this world rather than choosing to be clothed in Christ. *"Put on the Lord Jesus and make no provision for* the *flesh in regard to its lust"* (Romans 13:14). *"And put on the new self, which in the likeness of God has been created in righteousness and holiness of the truth"* (Ephesians 4:24).

Let us look more closely at the word *"by"* in the phrase *"by faith."* This word is a preposition, a pre-positioned word placed before a noun. This phrase informs us that faith is the means, the agent, of that which results in life situations. To speak of doing a thing "by faith," is to say faith is the instrument through which God has done or will do the change that is under discussion or observation. You who have faith continually, who are having God direct your life regularly, are living by faith.

Faith is one of God's most important creations. It is the door through which God does His saving and life giving work in us. In speaking about whether or not Gentile believers should observe the Law of Moses, Acts 15:8-9 reads, *"And God, who knows the heart, testified to them giving them the Holy Spirit, just as He also did to us; and He made no distinction between us and them, cleansing their hearts by* faith." Faith in Christ is a dynamic and powerful agent that first becomes the agent that cleanses our hearts; it opens our whole awareness to God and opens us to salvation. By that same faith, the power of the Spirit of God gives us what we need in order to obey. In addition, God's Spirit guides us on the path of the life that God planned for us.

Now, let us be clear about these marvelous wonders. These things do not occur in a mind that is open only to the "concept" of faith or the idea that faith is just some wonderful thing. Faith is an awakening to the adventure of life. Jesus is the prime motivator of everything we do in our lives, by faith. Faith is the

17: LIVING BY FAITH — PART I

agent that gives Jesus access into our hearts. You may want to review Part One at the beginning of this book where Matthew 9:29 is explained. There we see that Jesus healed two blind men *"according to their faith."* Magnificent and supernatural wonders along with healings occur in us and through us when we reach the point of realizing the power of the Holy Spirit in us as we live by faith. Living by faith activates God's Word. When we speak forth God's Word, as Jesus did, faith, mingled with God's promises, fulfills His word. Faith is the key that opens the lock to the realm of God's Kingdom. When you live and speak God's Word with unwavering faith, you are obeying God and following Jesus' example. You are walking in His footsteps. As we begin to live by faith, we will become assured in our hearts and minds, that this is the means by which Jesus will do His work through us. It is easy to understand that real faith is not some minor concept or some type of distant human philosophy. Actually, faith is life-transforming, life-enriching and life-giving power.

As we walk in faith, one treasure that results within us is God's peace. Peace is an increasing need in the Christian walk in times such as we live in today. When believers are alert, as we are called to be, we cannot help but compare our generation with things that are spoken of in the Bible regarding end times. See I Peter 1:20. Actually, we have been living in the end times ever since the ascension of Jesus Christ. The message that "Jesus is coming soon!" has been proclaimed among every generation since. The end times do seem to be coming closer as of late. Jesus spoke of it as being preceded by nations being at war and there being rumors of war. He said there would be

DOORWAYS to Greater Faith

famines, earthquakes, false teachings, love for Jesus and others would grow cold, increase of lawlessness, tribulation and death. See Matthew 24. Still, faith gives the faithful peace, even though we presently see the adversity as mentioned above. Living by faith in Jesus and knowing His care and love for us gives us great peace — a place of protection away from the cares of the world. Let the economy fail, let the nations attempt to repeat Babel and become a one-world nation. Let there be famines and droughts. Our Lord reigns, and through faith, you reign over these frightful situations also. Romans 5:17b reads, those who have the gift of faith *"will reign in life through the One, Jesus Christ."* We are quickly being brought to the place where we recognize, by faith, that God is truly our only security, our only hope.

God speaks more, saying, *"having been justified by faith, we have peace with God through our Lord Jesus Christ"* (Romans 5:1). Again, by faith, Jesus gives us peace in every imaginable situation. As world troubles continue and have now even entered many of our homes, Jesus tells us, *"These things I have spoken to you, so that in Me you may have peace. In the world you have tribulation, but take courage; I have overcome the world"* (John 16:33). In the same way that Jesus has overcome the world, we are those who overcome! This is our inheritance and we, again, accept this truth by faith. *"The just shall live by faith"* (Romans 1:17 KJV). How far do such wonders go in our lives? Enoch was translated by faith, so that he did not see death (Hebrews 11:5). Each believer can go as far in having

> *In the same way that Jesus has overcome the world, we are those who overcome by faith.*

17: LIVING BY FAITH — PART I

peace in their lives — as far as he or she will exercise faith in Jesus. It shall happen according to each believer's faith. Can you see why it is so important to understand about the power of faith? We can go as far as God originally planned for us to go by our own faith in Jesus. Paul spoke of God's plans for us that He made before He created the earth (Ephesians 1:4). Many love the verse Jeremiah 1:5, *"Before I formed thee in the belly I knew thee; and before thou camest forth out of the womb I sanctified thee, and I ordained thee a prophet unto the nations"* (KJV). As God did this for Jeremiah, He has unique plans for you. He knew you while you were in your mother's womb. He formed you there, planned for you there, and the plans were good (Jeremiah 29:11-13). We have been fearfully and wonderfully made. Let us live this by faith. As we do, God's purpose will be made complete in us as we surrender our lives to Him, daily.

We live in a world that is deceived into believing we can only exist by our own efforts; that we can endure by only what we possess. A particular car or home or job or business or religion represents our identity. God says, *"You stand by your faith"* (Romans 11:20). God is so adamant about our understanding faith that this truth is written in present tense so that we know the action is presently occurring in you as you read that truth. You stand by your faith! Your faith, in Christ, is the means by which you stand, how you persist and endure. By faith we make choices that are based on our focus on Christ. We must also guard our mind of faith. When our thoughts are impure, the Holy Spirit convicts us. Then, by faith, we turn our thoughts back to godly things. We refocus. God is so gracious. He even tells us, by faith, where to direct our minds. In Philippians 4:7, He shows us that the peace we have, by faith, guards our hearts and our minds in Christ Jesus. Then, He goes on to tell us, in detail, what will both guard and strengthen our minds: *"Finally brethren, whatever is true, whatever is honorable, whatever is right, whatever is pure, whatever is lovely, whatever is of good repute, if there is any excellence and if anything is worthy of praise, dwell on these things"* (Philippians 4:8). God continues by saying that through the practice of these things, the God of peace will be with you.

God says we are also to control our words of faith: *"Let no unwholesome word proceed from your mouth, but only such a word as is good for edification according to the need of the moment, so that it will give grace to those who hear"* (Ephesians 4:29). Faith has to do with the very words we speak to each other, and our own faith is lifted by the words we say to and about ourselves. We progress by believing God's Word, speaking it out and living it. Let us live by that faith now! As we live "by faith" we become increasingly aware of God working in our lives. We also become more responsive as He fills us with desire and passion to do the will of God in our lives by the great gift of faith. ✝

Study Questions:

1. What does "living by faith" mean to you?
2. Does the knowledge that Jesus stands behind your faith encourage you?
3. In what way has the Lord corrected or changed your mind and your words in how you respond to faith in your life?

17: LIVING BY FAITH — PART I

4. Has Jesus so filled your mind that, "by faith," you are beginning to recognize the words He speaks to you?
5. What is your response to living by faith? Are you ready to begin today? Do your words match up with your heart of faith?

CHAPTER 18

Living by Faith – Part Two
Various Bible Verses

You are so deeply loved by God that He invites you into His very life and fellowship. This is the most delightful place in the world to live. We have already seen in the parables of Matthew that being in His presence is like a pearl so valuable it is worth everything we own. It is the discovery and possession of this world's greatest treasure (Matthew 13:44-46). Experiencing God brings what we already knew to new light. We see new value that opens to us new treasures never before seen (Matthew 13:52).

This new relationship and greater wisdom concerning life, both this present life you live and the future life you shall live starts now, and it starts, yes, by faith. Faith casts fresh light and knowledge on all things.

As we age and live a life of increasing faith, we sometimes look back to our earlier life and wish we had the same wisdom

18: LIVING BY FAITH — PART II

then. In several more years, though, we'll be doing the same about today! We all feel that if we only knew then what we know now about the Lord..., but the point is that faith is so valuable for life, so valuable for knowing how to bless others and serve God that we invariably yearn to have known about it earlier in life. Those who are here know of what I am speaking.

Paul spoke repeatedly of such a yearning. He spoke of running the faith race *"in such a way that you may win"* (I Corinthians 9:24). He said we must not run this race in vain (Galatians 2:2). We must keep the faith (II Timothy 4:7) and press on to lay hold of everything for which Christ Jesus laid hold of him and us (Philippians 3:12). Faith is a response to the continued upward call of God in Christ Jesus. The life put before us in the Bible is to know and desire the deep things of faith. The author of the book of Hebrews said, *"run with endurance the race"* of faith in Jesus Christ (Hebrews 12:1).

A strong and solid foundation of faith is within your grasp. You will find, if you don't already know, that it can be easily understood. Small children understand the concept of faith. Faith is the means by which God includes you in His plans. What a delightful word it becomes in the minds of the faithful. It is the means through which God spans the space between the visible and the invisible.

> *Faith is the means through which God spans the space between the visible and the invisible.*

Paul, in his own experience, helps us to see more clearly between faith as just a concept of a religiously inclined person and faith that is the vital, life enabling faith given by God that is powered by the Spirit of God. Paul's faith began as just religion, which is man's effort to find God. Religion is man at work for the purpose of finding God. One aspect of faith is that it reveals God at work to find man. Paul received his education from his teacher, Gamaliel, a highly ranked doctor of Jewish Law (Acts 22:3).

Paul was well known for his knowledge and zealous adherence to the Jewish Law, and was himself a well-known teacher of the Law. He had a huge problem, however. Though he was one of the most highly educated men in Israel about the things of God, he did not know God. He had never met Jesus until he was on the road to Damascus.

A true knowledge of Jesus actually is what the Bible refers to when it speaks of faith. Faith is personal and intimate and settles a person into knowledge of Jesus as loving Savior, Brother and Friend. God, in order to make that higher spiritual knowledge more understandable to us, compared that kind of knowledge to a man's love for the girl who would become his wife. This refers to his love and yearning for her, and holds no sexual connotations.

> *Faith is a personal and intimate knowledge of Jesus.*

There is love that transcends the earthly and this is it. It is what we all long to find, and once we do, there is no turning back. This reference is found in Ephesians 5:31-32. It is a glad and joyful, *"I can't live without you"* yearning, an *"I must have you with me always"* knowledge, a realization that *"you make me love life."* This is a knowing where your heart awakens, and you reach for that person and grasp hold, and hold on the rest of your life with all that is within you — forever. You can't

18: LIVING BY FAITH — PART II

imagine living without that person. Faith is an awakened awareness of Who God is and you cannot even imagine living without Him.

One day, on the road to Damascus (Acts 9:1-5), Jesus met the "religious" Paul. Paul was startled: *"Who are You, Lord?"* Did you notice that Paul called Him *"Lord?"* He already knew Jesus. The presence of God is recognizable, even to those who do not have faith. What we see here is a tough, trained mind going through some preliminary breaking down of fallacy to find truth. Paul's heart and mind were **rushed through the straightening out process** and met up with faith, face to face. You have felt such an untangling process in your own thoughts before over some surprising truth. Such an untangling happened to me once when I had been traveling east on Long Island, New York. My internal GPS told me that I was, in fact — definitely traveling east! Suddenly, I realized, because of the landmarks, that my internal GPS was completely wrong. I was, actually, in fact — definitely traveling west! It felt as if my brain ripped loose and turned around in my head. That was what Paul was experiencing. This mind of Paul that knew so much *about* God, finally met God — met Jesus Christ up close and personal. His heart and mind were **ripped open by the faith giver Himself** and Jesus poured Himself upon Paul. Paul chose faith!

"By faith, we understand that the worlds were prepared by the Word of God, so that what is seen was not made out of things which are visible" (Hebrews 11:3). This knowledge leap connects two realities making our understanding of faith more clear. God went so far as to say creation itself reveals the knowledge of

God's existence, making those who refuse Him responsible for their lack of faith. *"That which is known about God is evident within them; for God made it evident to them. For since the creation of the world His invisible attributes, His eternal power and divine nature, have been clearly seen, being understood through what has been made, so that they are without excuse"* (Romans 1:19-20).

This thought continues in Romans Chapter One stating that, though they knew God through the creation, they did not honor God or give thanks, so God let their refusal of Him darken their minds. Faith can bring light to darkened minds, but to those who choose darkness, He lets them go. Faith also is the agent that God uses to connect us to His plans and purposes for our lives. We see it in Noah: *"By faith Noah, being warned by God concerning events as yet unseen, in reverent fear, constructed an ark for the saving of his household. By this, he condemned the world and became an heir of the righteousness that comes by faith"* (Hebrews 11:7 ESV).

God's plans for us include our being made just or righteous. His plans include us having peace and right or correct actions in all circumstances. That is a good definition of righteousness. He made it possible for us to be able to stand firm in all of His grace.

Therefore, He said through Paul, "having *been justified by faith, we have peace with God through our Lord Jesus Christ, through whom also we have access by faith into this grace in which we stand; and we exult in hope of the glory of God"* (Romans 5:1-2). Faith is the instrument that brings us into that relationship with God where we know more of His grace and righteousness. Peace then fills and strengthens us.

18: LIVING BY FAITH — PART II

We have come to an important understanding of our faith in that God imparts to the faithful His ability to work humanly impossible miracles through us. Sarah received strength to conceive Isaac at age ninety, well past the age of childbearing (Hebrews 11:11).

Peter, by faith, prayed and got instructions from God to raise the body of Tabitha from the dead (Acts 9:40). By faith, you have prayed and have had your sick child healed, and have had them and others you prayed for surrender to Jesus Christ as their Savior and Lord. Recently, I had a man tell me his wife prayed for him all their life. She fell ill with cancer. Later, he told me he watched his faithful wife, who loved Jesus, die. He said the manner of death, as she held to Jesus, brought him to faith in Christ.

Remember Jesus' instruction in our Chapter Eight is that we are to recall our past experiences in which He revealed His power to us. In those times you have prayed for help and wonderful things have happened. Write them down so you can remember them. The miracles and healings we read of in the Bible are also to be made manifest through your life. They are presently occurring in other Christians both here and in other countries. Such activity is possible in any Christian, "by faith."

God tells us that signs and wonders will follow us. He gives people every opportunity to be used in this manner. His wonderful works, through us, are to be a conduit for the dying world to see Him and His glory. As signs and wonders were needed for unbelievers in the Bible, they are needed for unbelievers in every generation, including this one. It is all done by faith. God's plan is for Jesus to use individual, faith-filled, believers the same way He used Jesus. Jesus laid aside His privileges as God to become human so that we could see how God wants "living by faith" to be done. That is our place, to be like Jesus and live by faith just as He did. Because it is done by faith and we have so many other examples in God's Word as well, we know that this life of faith is possible and advantageous for us and for those around us.! ✝

Study Questions:

1. What is the difference between religion and faith?
2. What is the difference between intellectual knowledge of God and a personal relationship with God?
3. In what way does understanding that faith is an instrument, a means for God to access you through Jesus Christ help you understand faith?
4. What are some of the plans that you believe God has for your life? Pray and allow time for you to hear His voice and what He wants from you.
5. What do you believe are your next steps in exercising faith as you live your life by faith?

CHAPTER 19

FAITH AND GOOD PEOPLE
Acts 10

There are people we would call "good' all around us. Most of us have some good neighbors, we see kindness in people, and there are individuals who go out of their way to help others in need. We know many good people we consider good friends.

Here is one account of a good person in the Bible: Cornelius. Cornelius was a Roman military officer in command of a hundred men. He respected and had affection for others. The Bible called him *"devout."* He was religious. He and his household respected God and gave gifts of charity to the Jewish community. The Jews of Caesarea all spoke well of Cornelius, calling him a righteous and God-fearing man. The messengers Cornelius sent to Peter called Cornelius *"a righteous and God-fearing man well spoken of by the entire nation of the Jews"* (Acts 10:22).

DOORWAYS to Greater Faith

He prayed continuously. God said his prayers and gifts of charity ascended as a memorial before God (verse 4). Incidentally, did anyone ever say God does not hear people pray before they become believers, or that the first prayer God hears is the prayer for salvation? Notice what the Bible teaches us about this as we proceed. What else did such a man need to offer beside continuous prayer and gifts of charity? Many Churches would gladly accept him into membership and place him in a leadership or teaching position, especially in classes about prayer and tithing and caring for the poor. He was an excellent example of the goodness that we as Christians should exemplify. Some would consider Cornelius an excellent prospect for an office in the Church because he exhibited such consistent goodness.

What does God have to say about such a man? Cornelius was living his life as a good, God-fearing man. He talked to God regularly. He was involved in the kind of living and caring God wants to see in His children. Only, that wasn't enough. We need to be careful about falling into this same trap of being content with ourselves because we look good and do good. Loving God, believing in God, and even doing good deeds are not enough. Giving gifts of charity is not enough. Praying alone is not enough. Loving on a city full of people is not enough. Cornelius knew God through the strict Jewish faith. They believed, as many do today, that they were saved through the Law, saved by the works they did. Doing these things because we know God wants us to do them does not save us. Rather than working out "ways" that are customary and comfortable for us, hear this truth: God wants our

19: FAITH AND GOOD PEOPLE

heart, our whole heart, all of it. He wants total surrender. Too often, we focus on our deeds, on what we want to accomplish. God wants you focused on loving Him whole-heartedly. Such a love refocuses our whole life correctly. Then God, having our whole heart, surrendered to Him, will lead us into the work we are created to do, the love and kindness and worship we should offer. Hear God's Word as it reaches into the depths of our heart. God addresses this to our generation: *"I will give them a heart to know Me, for I am the Lord; and they will be My people, and I will be their God, for they will return to Me with their whole heart"* (Jeremiah 24:7). Paul wrote to the church at Galatia: *"Nevertheless knowing that a man is not justified (made righteous) by the works of the law, but through faith in Christ Jesus, even we have believed in Christ Jesus, so that we may be justified by faith in Christ and not by works of the law; since by the works of the law no flesh will be justified"* (Galatians 2:16).

> ... *good and religious people must come to Jesus by faith.*

Toward the end of his life of mighty works for the Lord Jesus, Paul said, *"I count all things to be loss in view of the surpassing value of knowing Christ Jesus my Lord, for whom I have suffered the loss of all things, and count them but rubbish so that I may gain Christ"* (Philippians 3:8). You see, what we do — as in goodness — has nothing to do with our salvation. Such activity can lull and deceive the best of people, leading them away from true faith. Therefore, we read about Cornelius, a man so good that a city full of people loved him, that God sent an angel to speak to him. *"About the ninth hour of the day (three o'clock in the afternoon) he clearly saw in a vision an angel of God who had just*

DOORWAYS to Greater Faith

come in and said to him, 'Cornelius!' (Acts 10:3). *"Your prayers and alms have ascended as a memorial before God. Now dispatch some men to Joppa and send for a man named Peter"* (Acts 10:4-5). God sent an angel to a man who believed in God but who did not understand the concept of true salvation! God hears the prayers of people who are not His own, just as he had heard Cornelius.

The Bible speaks of many who fell out of God's graces because of pride in their own works. Many heathens prayed and were heard by God, including Nebuchadnezzar, and the Pharaoh of Egypt, but let us get back to Cornelius. We see God's mercy upon Cornelius when the angel tells him to hear a message from Peter (Acts 10:22). This good man needed more information about God than he had. God wanted to give Cornelius every opportunity to receive the truth. With all his commitment and works, he did not understand the true message of salvation, and God sent Peter to liberate him from his false understanding. Many wonderful people are still caught up in good intentions, yet they have not received the true message of salvation and surrendered their hearts. Such people are not aware, as Cornelius was not, that they have become dangerous to themselves. Watch Cornelius. He was hungry for God's truth. Add to that the truth that he had a vision and saw an angel, a fact so amazing and unexpected, and little known, that he called the angel, *"Lord."* He thought he was talking to God. He was so hungry for spiritual truth he thought the angel was God. The angel told him he needed to hear a message from Peter; here's his address. *"Send for him!"* Cornelius did. Arriving at Cornelius' house, Peter entered and Cornelius fell

19: FAITH AND GOOD PEOPLE

at his feet and worshiped him. When people are spiritually hungry, they tend to worship whatever or whoever sounds good or right to them. They had good intentions, but were still wrong. That's how religion, cults, drug addiction and witchcraft become so enticing.

Cornelius was ready to worship even Peter in his zeal to worship. Peter pulled Cornelius to his feet saying, "*Stand up; I too am just a man*" (Acts 10:26). Peter gave Cornelius and those with him the message of God. He said, "God has shown me that He does not show partiality." In other words, Jesus welcomes Jews and Gentiles alike, those we consider good and those we even consider bad. Jesus welcomes mistaken people who are ready to repent, and those who fear Him and want to do what is right. They are ripe for the harvest and hearing the truth of God's salvation plan. The word God has for every one is the gospel of peace through Jesus Christ (Acts 10:35-36). He spoke to Cornelius, and those with him, of Jesus' works: His healings, His death on the cross, His resurrection. Peter told them that all who believe in Him receive forgiveness of sins. The wonderful and amazing thing about God's word is that during this very time, all who were listening believed and were filled with the Holy Spirit. God's word still has the power to move people in the same way today.

Looking into this facet of faith, which is about <u>Faith and Good People</u>, we see that everyone needs to be introduced to Jesus. If we do not tell others about Jesus, their spiritual hunger may open them up to worship anything and anyone. Then, too, they are anxious to please anyone they think is God who exhibits supernatural ability versus worshiping Jesus Himself who gives the power. They will actually worship such men and women. This is happening through out the world today. It is even happening in some Churches. There are those who are just good natured people. There are those who are just bad natured people. The darkness in both groups and any other group can be penetrated by the message of faith in Jesus Christ. All of us, no matter how good or bad, need to hear the word of faith, faith in Jesus Christ. He saves us, and it is not by our church membership, goodness or any good works. God loves us so much, He sent His Son Jesus Christ. Only faith in Jesus saves us. Any religious activity outside of faith in Jesus Christ can be a danger and deception to true faith. Jesus Christ must be the focus of our life and living. Jesus considered the pious, religious leaders of his time, *"whitewashed tombs,"* because they had no faith in Jesus and the Messiah to back their knowledge of God. Jesus said, *"The time is fulfilled, and the Kingdom of God is at hand* (right now); *repent and believe in the gospel"* (Mark 1:15 — in parentheses, mine). Jesus said, *"Follow Me"* (Mark 1:17). We must walk after Him; have a continuing personal relationship with Jesus. That is what following Jesus means. It gives purpose and meaning to our lives. Being a good person does not complete us. Knowing Jesus and living like Him, does. ☨

STUDY QUESTIONS:

1. How can a person be good and still not understand God's truth about salvation?

19: FAITH AND GOOD PEOPLE

2. How is being good related to faith? Does being good about religious activity get one to heaven?

3. If you are married, engaged or have found the love of your life, can you equate this with how you give your whole heart to God?

4. What steps does God ask us to follow to ensure our salvation versus just being a "good" person?

CHAPTER 20

FAITH AND DREAMS
Acts 2:14–21

God gives us the gift of dreams. Dreams are mentioned in eighteen books of the Bible as one of God's ways of communicating with mankind; unbelievers as well as believers. Considering the importance of God communicating with us, and how we must position ourselves to receive dreams, dreams are a subject worthy of consideration as we study faith.

In the New Testament, the word for dream, *enupnion*, means "a vision in sleep." It refers to a supernatural impression or suggestion received during sleep. Acts 2:17 speaks of old men dreaming dreams. When we consider this Biblical truth, it is good and wise to study what God wants us to understand about dreams.

The Bible calls dreams, "*night visions*" in Isaiah 29:7. On his second missionary journey, Paul had such a night vision. He

20: FAITH AND DREAMS

and his companions were trying to take the Gospel into the cities of Bithynia, but *"the Spirit of Jesus did not permit them"* (Acts 16:7). You can imagine their consternation as they attempted to go there and various circumstances prevented them each time. Finally, we are told in Acts 16:9 that *"A vision appeared to Paul in the night: a man of Macedonia was standing and appealing to him, and saying, 'Come over to Macedonia and help us.'"*

In Acts 16:10 we read where he and those with him concluded that God had called them to preach the gospel in Macedonia. Apparently, they had prayed for guidance, and Paul relayed his dream vision to them. They all recognized the voice of God in the dream as instruction for where God wanted them to go instead of Bithynia.

This supernatural gift of dreams, that comes to us more than we realize, is spelled out for us in Job 33:14-17: *"Indeed God speaks once, or twice, yet no one notices it. In a dream, a vision of the night, when sound sleep falls on men, while they slumber in their beds, then He opens the ears of men, and seals their instruction, that He may turn man aside from his conduct (his actions good or bad) and keep man from pride."*

> *Friend, by faith, we expect God to be moving and dealing with us in personal ways. He goes so far as to touch us while we are sleeping and nudge us onward with dreams and visions.*

Dream visions seem to be necessary at times when our lives are too full of other distractions. In seeing the group work together in the interpretation of Paul's dream in Acts 16:10, one wonders how much revelation Christians might be missing today when this aspect of God's communication is misunderstood, ignored, or not believed. When we study dreams, we are not talking about some truth that the Bible carefully places in some corner to be ignored or neglected. Scripture speaks of dreams 112 times in 18 books. The understanding of the importance of dreams is widely accepted and understood in a vast number of Biblical accounts. It is highly recognized in the Word as one of God's means to communicate. He uses this means to speak to believers and non-believers alike. When Jesus was presented to the court, Pontius Pilate was faced with the dilemma of convicting what he believed was an innocent man. It upset him and his wife even came to him and told her husband that she had a dream about this man and his importance. Pontius Pilate then gave the decision over to the people and they chose to let Barnabas go free and to crucify Jesus. As far as we know, Pontius Pilate's wife was not a follower of Jesus, but God had given her a dream – a warning. Her husband was wise to listen.

The important point here is that God really is in charge, and we are blessed when He comes to us while we are sleeping. There He opens our ears and seals, or impresses His truth in our minds and spirits. At that point we become responsible to approach God in prayer, to ask for further understanding concerning what He has said to us.

Notice two things here, dreamers: This says dreams are to change our actions and also to keep us from pride. Dreams are not meant to point us to the dreamer as if he or she is some spiritual giant. Dreams point us to people who are in need as God directs. Primarily, however, dreams point us to God who *may* have spoken to us through that dream! We always want to

20: FAITH AND DREAMS

pay attention when God speaks to us. We want to understand all He has for us. Jesus said He speaks to His sheep – all of them! John 10:27 says, *"My sheep hear My voice, and I know them, and they follow Me."* Isn't this wonderful! God speaks to you. God does not reserve His communication for some super elite religious group. As Jesus did when He was on the earth, God speaks to all who will listen. The interpretation of dreams in the situation with Paul was a group process. When a group works together there is no limelight for one individual, therefore pride is eliminated.

The Gospel is for the world. It reaches to all and therefore has to be opened to all. Pharaoh had a dream from God about a coming famine (Genesis 41:7). King Nebuchadnezzar *saw* a dream (Daniel 4:1,2). Then God gave Daniel the interpretation (Daniel 2:36ff). Now ponder on the wonder of this: That dream reached into the future, covering the coming history of Babylon, the Medo-Persian Empire, Greece, Rome and the future Kingdom of God for which you and I are waiting. It covered hundreds of years.

The Lord appeared to Solomon in a dream (I Kings 3:5). He appeared to Joseph in a dream, saying, *"Joseph, son of David, do not be afraid to take Mary as your wife; for the Child who has been conceived in her is of the Holy Spirit"* (Matthew 1:20). It seems that dreams have had a valuable place in history and continue to do so – for those who will listen.

Sometimes I wonder how many inventions have come to mankind through dreams. We cannot be so blind to think that God cannot use this means of communication. Sometimes dreams are vivid. In Judges 7:13-15, Gideon heard a man relaying his dream to a friend, and bowed in worship and returned to his camp saying, "*Arise, for the Lord has given the camp of Midian into your hands.*" He knew that the dream he had heard his enemy recounting to a friend was God's message for him to attack his enemy.

God speaks to us in the way He chooses. As you walk more closely with God on a daily basis, you will find this to be true for yourself. The ways He communicates with each of us is as unique as our own personality. God chooses the things that will touch our hearts and open our minds to what He is asking and/or saying. I choose, by faith, to believe what God says about dreams and about how He speaks to all of us. Like you, I want God to speak to me. If I'm having trouble opening my ears to His voice while awake, I invite Him to speak to me in my sleep. I yearn to hear God.

As we continue our discussion about dreams, let us get personal about it. How many of us have awakened from a dream and immediately move into earnest prayer for the person we dreamed about? Many of us have. How many have been called in a dream to pray for specific people in your church — or for your city, or for the nation? I believe this is a normal practice and calling for God's people. God is a supernatural God who works in supernatural ways. Anything is possible with God so we need to be open to the ways He reaches into our lives to communicate with us. Some errantly may think dreams are only for those persons we imagine are closer to the Lord or for those who are ultra-spiritual – anyone but us! Listen to me. You are God's chosen. Jesus did say all things are possible for us, by our faith in Him. Those words are for you as much as they are

20: FAITH AND DREAMS

for those we admire for their stand on faith. Dreams are for the known faithful as well as for the unknown. Some of the people who were considered, "nobodies" in their time, are mentioned in the Bible as receiving communication from God via dreams – and for standing in faith believing those dreams. They are some of the ones God chooses because He knows they are open to listening for His voice in this manner. That means that he can, does, and will choose us if we let Him. Think of the nameless faces of faithful people who have brought Christianity to our generation.

Who is Enoch, really? Do we really ever get a full biography of Enoch? Who are Prochorus, Nicanor, Timon, Pharmenas, and Nicolas mentioned in Acts 6:5? Who are the four virgin daughters of Philip, who prophesied? They are, just like us, the unknowns. God is not looking for famous people of notoriety or people who are revered by all. He is looking for those who abandon the rational to believe in the supernatural wonders of God. We are all such an intricate part of God's plan that He sacrificed His Son Jesus Christ, for us. God says that He uses the simple to confound the wise. Paul admonished Timothy, who was a very young preacher, to exercise his authority. Paul told Timothy not to consider himself as being inadequate because of his youth. Lest you believe that you are not important, God considered Moses to be the most humble man who every existed. He had a problem with stuttering, yet God chose him to go before Pharaoh and tell Pharaoh that God wanted His people set free! Today, we are His followers. God wants us set free. Let us consider an important concern here regarding dreams and their interpretation. If we make a mistake interpreting a dream, understand that it is better than not trying to hear from God at all in this way. God is patient with us. He will help us as we continue working with Him to hear His voice in dreams and visions that He gives. God rewards our faith. He can use our mistakes to keep us humble. We need each other and we can confirm each other's faith as we come together in these things. We will make mistakes in any task we head out to tackle. The point is that we try, learn and, eventually, clearly hear God in such ways as He gives them to us. God will always confirm His Word by two or three witnesses, so you can always be sure that if a dream interpretation is given about you or for you, you can wait on God to confirm it. He will.

> *If we make a mistake interpreting a dream, understand that it is better than not trying to hear from God at all in this way. God is patient with us. He will help us.*

We need to listen to God more carefully, with more expectancy, and be ready to press even further into and with God. Our Lord Jesus did. Paul did, "*I press on,*" Paul said in Philippians 3:14. "*I press on toward the goal for the prize of the upward call of God in Christ Jesus.*" Well, let *us* press on, too. Remember that we are to be caught up in Christ and not in the sensationalism of our dream or dreams. The Lord is to be our focus, not His tools for communicating with us.

We should not confine God with our limited understanding as we open and respond to His Word. He is the One who gives dreams. He is the one urging us forward in our faith. He is trying to help us, and, as Job says, He is helping us through dreams when things in our waking lives are too hectic for us

20: FAITH AND DREAMS

being able to hear Him clearly. He understands our problems, and right where we are, He finds us and helps us. He does love us so!

For years, I thought all my dreams were about others, regardless of who I saw in the dreams and regardless of what they did. I never considered that God was trying to communicate with me about my own life. Once again, I was wrong. Many dreams are God communicating to the one dreaming. Some dreams are stirrings from the events of the day. Others dreams are stirrings from the dinner we had before we went to sleep. Sometimes, the Lord shows us that it is time to get rid of sin in our lives. Sometimes, as the Bible states, God may use dreams to reveal that significant change is about to take place. Joseph dreamed he would rule over his brothers as we read in the story about Joseph's life in Genesis 37:6-8. It surely happened.

In some of our dreams, the Lord will reveal spiritual mistakes we make. One time I had a flash vision/dream of someone's shirttail being caught by the hands of another. It was so startling that it awakened me. As I prayed for the interpretation, I realized it was a dream vision – the kind of instantaneous communication that comes from God in quick flashes. The next morning, I continued to pray for the interpretation and realized the vision was about me. As I continued to pray, I believe the Lord told me that I was holding on to my own shirttail. I felt that there was more to this, so I continued praying for the complete message to be revealed. I had been holding myself back from growing in faith. My own hands were clutching my own shirttail prohibiting me from moving forward. God took three days to reveal the entire interpretation to me. As the Holy Spirit brings us into all truth, as God promises, we sense incompletion and are prompted to pray further regarding some things in our lives. We must be open and pliable for God to work with us – not closing our hearts and minds to His working in us. Some interesting results followed this dream that significantly affected my growth.

There may be times when God gives us dreams about our Church or a friend, and sometimes, even a stranger. Be careful not to ignore your dreams, as they may be more important than you realize. God confirms many things that he has already said to us and to others through our dreams. Your dream may be the very confirmation someone needs in order to move forward toward his or her destiny. This is the depth of importance in following God's lead regarding the matter of our dreams and visions that He gives us.

When God gives us personal messages through our dreams, we don't always need an outside interpretation. That is how my dream vision worked regarding my allowing growth in the area of faith for my life. God gave me the dream/vision and the interpretation through much prayer. This is acceptable, but if dreams are about someone else, they may need to receive additional confirmation from others regarding that dream to establish the truth in it for their own lives. If you give someone else an interpretation for their dream and they seem to ignore you, have patience and pray that the Lord will give them that second and/or third witness to establish the truth in what God has shown you. This goes back to the concept that we all work together as a team. Iron sharpens iron as we help each other

20: FAITH AND DREAMS

through this life. Some dreams are God's messages to us. Friends, *by faith* we expect God to be moving and dealing with us, especially in such very personal ways. He goes so far as to touch us while we are sleeping and nudge us onward in our dreams and visions. Who would have ever thought that God would go to such lengths to be so personal with us? We know, by His love and expansive array of methods of communication to us that we are His beloved children.

Again, let me express that we don't get so sidetracked by the sensationalism of dreams/visions and interpretation of them that we disrupt and confuse our lives and the lives of others. Our spiritual stability in Jesus Christ, through the power of the Holy Spirit, is very fragile, and He works with us without causing confusion. We must be aware that God speaks to us in dreams and visions, but not worship the ways God communicates to us. We listen and enjoy all He has to say to us in whatever manner He chooses to reach out to us and keep God the center focus of our lives always.

Study Questions:

1. What does it mean to you that God is the same yesterday, today, and forever as you regard how God communications to us in dreams and visions?
2. Are you willing to start exercising faith in this area? Have you had dreams and visions from the Lord? Ask God what the dreams and visions mean and wait for his exciting answer. If it involves others, pray for your answers together.

3. How does it make you feel that God touches us in such a personal and loving way while we sleep?
4. Do you expect God to move and deal with you in the personal ways we have examined in this chapter?

CHAPTER 21

FAITH AND MENTAL ATTITUDES
Philippians 4:4–9

We have touched on the importance of guarding your mind and how fear is the opposite of faith. In this chapter, we will examine the word, *guard*, and the phrase, *fear not*, more closely. For instance, I sincerely believe you, the reader, are probably much farther down the road of faith than you imagine right now. As you have been exploring about your faith in the first twenty chapters of this book, you are continuing to read with interest regarding how to better allow God to open the doors of faith before you. What does He have for your life? God knows the sincerity of our hearts, but we suffer with attitude problems that inhibit our belief system. Somewhere along the way of faith, we have misunderstood God's ways toward us. We have allowed the enemy to cloud our judgment resulting in condemning attitudes toward ourselves. The Spirit, whose intent is to continually point us into Christ's ways, corrects us. We know God is on our side as He does this.

The Bible clearly tells us that it is up to us to guard our minds. *Guard* means to *keep watch*. Jesus said: "*He who loves his life loses it, and he who hates* (regards with less affection) *his life in this world will keep* (guard) *it to life eternal*" (John 12:25 – in parentheses, mine). We keep our new minds focused properly by turning our attention upon Jesus. Everyone is capable of guarding their mind.

Jesus released us from worry. Have you ever considered what this means for the renewing of your mind? If we would truly learn to keep from worry, what joy we would experience. If only we would cast all of our cares on Him. Jesus said this, "*I say to you, 'do not be worried about your life...*" "*Seek first His Kingdom and His righteousness and all these things will be added to you*" (Matthew 6:25,33). Notice Jesus' assurance, "*all these things will be added to you.*" They will be provided! God will take care of those things that you worry about. The awesome wonder of this is that this kind of peaceful existence is already ours! Our responsibility is to accept our gift.

Picking up on this again, Paul says, "*Be anxious for nothing*" (Philippians 4:6). God even tells us how to melt away our worry and anxiety. He said, "*Rejoice in the Lord always; again I will say, rejoice*" (Philippians 4:4)! Well, how can we rejoice when we don't feel like it? I understand this. Any person who has walked the Christian walk for more than a day understands this. We've all been here, but let me tell you that this mindset of freedom is possible, because as negative as I used to

21: FAITH AND MENTAL ATTITUDES

be, it has worked for me. It's called giving *"a sacrifice of praise"* in Hebrews 13:15. We do it in faith. We just do it! Why do we have our pity parties and want to question God about everything rather than trusting Him? I once heard a preacher say to someone who was worrying: "Just die." His abruptness shocked me until I took some time to consider the truth behind this. We must die to our own selfish wishes, even the desire to have a pity party, and turn to Jesus. As we remember what He did for us, we can thank Him. As we move through this life, we know our salvation is sure because of Jesus. Praise Him! You will be amazed at the healing qualities this sacrifice of praise will bring you.

Remember that we are talking about guarding our minds, about stopping certain thoughts and attitudes at the door of our minds, and refusing their entrance, or greasing their exit if they are already inside. When Jesus was tempted, He quoted God's Word to rid Himself of the temptation.

Here is a perfect guard position for our minds: *"Rejoice in the Lord ... again: rejoice! ...Be anxious for nothing ... pray ... supplicate ... with thanksgiving let your request be made known to God."* When we do that, and rejoice and thank God and celebrate until this happens, God said, *"the peace of God, which surpasses all com-*

> *Part of faith is learning to guard your thoughts as Jesus did. Let the Word push out the Tempter's thoughts from your mind.*

prehension will guard your hearts and your minds in Christ Jesus." See Philippians 4:7. It worked for Paul. It works for you. God gives peace to you. You can't get it on your own! God does it. We are not responsible to try to create peace with ourselves.

DOORWAYS to Greater Faith

God is responsible because He told us it works. Furthermore, He will give you peace that surpasses all comprehension when you turn to Him with faith. That in itself gives us peace and joy, too!

As long as you, guard your thoughts. Jesus Christ will wrap your mind in His peace. *"Peace I leave with you; My peace I give to you; not as the world gives do I give to you. Do not let your heart* (mind) *be troubled, nor let it be fearful"* (John 14:27 — in parentheses, mine). Child of God, notice in this verse that you are responsible to guard your own mind. Meld your thoughts with Jesus' thoughts so your thoughts will become one with His. He prayed that we would be one with Him. Let it happen. Over and again, Jesus told His disciples, *"fear not."* When God is in control, there is nothing to fear. Remember that God is with you. What need do we have to fear?

There is a reason Jesus repeatedly urged believers to have no fear. The angel of God told Zacharias to fear not. The angel told Mary to fear not. The angel told the shepherds who saw the great star in the sky, to, *"be not afraid."* When Jesus instructed the fisherman, Peter, where to throw his nets to make a catch, He told him to fear not at his enormous catch of fish. Do not fear the miracles, either. We do not need to fear the supernatural beauty of God and His gifts to us.

In each of the above situations, God has a message He wants us to hear. Zacharias, after years of wanting a child, was, at last, going to have a baby. His child with his elderly wife was none other than the great messenger who told of the coming Messiah. Mary was going to give birth to Jesus. The shepherds were going to see the Holy Child, the long awaited

21: FAITH AND MENTAL ATTITUDES

King of Kings. Peter was going to become a fisher of men, a disciple of the same Messiah. If those who were hearing these miraculous announcements out of heaven had become fearful, their minds would have been unable to accept the subsequent call on their lives. Fear blocks the mind. It disables our faith. It is the opposite of faith. Just like a negative cannot equal a positive, so fear cannot equal faith, ever! Fear prevents us from hearing God's words, blocking our communication to our Father. It blocks what God is doing in our lives, and it is a powerful weapon of the devil, our enemy. It can be only as useful to our enemy as we let it be, though our fear. Fear is a spiritual attack upon the believer, and we face this tactic of the enemy every day. If we turn our back on fear, it cannot exist. The key: Turn our backs on fear and turn our eyes to Jesus. Again, if we resist the devil, he *will* flee from us. Faith and fear cannot coexist. Fear not!

One last thing we need to discuss in this chapter is the importance of guarding our words. Our words are mighty. Once a word is spoken, it speeds to its mark. It is wise for us to think before we speak as our words are the seeds planted for our own future. Jesus will give us wisdom to know what to speak, when to speak and when not to speak. In the middle of a sentence I have heard His voice, in my own heart, tell me to stop and not even finish the sentence I was in the middle of speaking. You, too, as you follow Jesus, hear His voice. You have been speaking and realize you should not say what you are about to speak. That is God communicating His will and wisdom to you! He is prompting you to do what is right. Each time, we have the opportunity to make that instant decision to obey or disobey. When we obey and stop what we were about to say, or were in process of saying, it encourages other believers around us to do the same. It also shows non-believers the sincerity of our walk with God and how God does guide us. It is amazing how God uses even these small decisions to help others. Guarding our attitudes, our words and our minds often requires lightning quick — instant decisions. Each time, we are responsible. Each time God is communicating His will to you and guiding you with His wisdom. Every believer hears the Father's voice and has the opportunity to obey or disobey in these situations. We must understand how our decisions and our words effect our present situations, our future and others around us.

Regarding our words, God says, *"Let no unwholesome (rotten) word proceed from your mouth, but only such a word as is good for edification according to the need of the moment, so that it will give grace to those who hear"* (Ephesians 4:29). Remember, "grace" is a favor that is not earned by the one receiving it.

The Lord is at work instructing us through our minds. These are faithful ways we can respond. There is a wonderful secret in all of this. If we keep our minds focused on learning more about Jesus, the way we need to think becomes increasingly clear. We recognize when a thought is wrong and this recognition process happens more swiftly as we grow. As we learn about Jesus in God's Word and listen to the voice of the Father, He leads by the power of the Holy Spirit, and we become more and more like Jesus every day. This gives us such great hope!

"Finally, brethren, whatever is true, whatever is honorable, whatever is right, whatever is pure, whatever is lovely, whatever is of good

21: FAITH AND MENTAL ATTITUDES

repute, if there is any excellence and if anything worthy of praise, dwell on these things" (Philippians 4:8). Practice these things, Paul said, and the God of peace will be with you. ✝

STUDY QUESTIONS:

1. Have you been a person who worries? In what ways do your worries choke out the promises you have from God?
2. What is the importance of not worrying?
3. How do we go about guarding our minds and our words?
4. Remember a time, in your own mind, when God told you not to continue something you were saying and you decided to obey. To keep those hurtful words from being spoken when God specifically told you not to speak them, acknowledging that you have had these experiences is enough for this discussion. Talk together about *how* God communicated to you, the importance of listening and acting quickly. You can do this without revealing what He told you not to say.
5. What revelation about your faith and mental attitude have you received in this study?

Part Three
Living by Faith

"But the righteous man shall live by faith."
(Romans 1:17)

PART THREE

TO LIVE BY FAITH
Hebrews 10:38

What an adventure and privilege it is to be called to live by faith! We, who believe in Jesus, are called to live in a way that is completely opposite from everything most others ever experience. We contradict many things we have learned. We are new beings who have been called by God to enter into the experience of being His children. From the time we are the children of our earthly parents', they teach us to take care of ourselves. Being a child of God means learning to let God take care of you. We must release our self-reliance and depend upon our Heavenly Father, exclusively. As you can see, this goes against all we are taught. I'm reminded of Peter trembling as He watched Jesus walking on the water. At Peter's bold statement: *"Lord, if it is You, command me to come to You on the water,"* Jesus said, *"Come!"* Quickly, and without hesitation, Peter stood on the edge of adventure. In a similar way we stand on that edge, hearing the echo of God's call for us to live by faith. We must remember

DOORWAYS to Greater Faith

that even when we stumble, Jesus will catch our hand. Fear should never prohibit us from stepping out in our life by faith in what God calls us to do. How do we do this? Do it boldly! God said, *"My righteous one shall live by faith."* We step out into all that our new life calls us to experience. The grammar in this verse suggests that walking by faith is a fact. Our righteousness moves us into this walk. Jesus had already told us through the Apostle John that we have the right to do just that. It is so because, just as Jesus lived by faith, we now have His ability and His power to move us through what He gives us to do. What a privilege! It is to walk in His righteousness, free from fear and bold in faith.

> *Faith launches us into Jesus Christ's Words, promises and life.*

A few moments ago, I was praying about what to say in this introductory statement to Part Three, "To Live by Faith." As I prayed, I reached forward and asked God to help me to open all the doors of faith that God originally designed for us to understand here. We know He wants our faith to be equal to Jesus' faith. He had all of our lives planned before He ever created anything, before the foundation of the world. *"He chose us in Him before the foundation of the world"* (Ephesians 1:4). You can walk knowing that God has before ordained all that He has set in place for you to walk out. You are able to walk in faith, knowing that our loving Father, God, prepared the way. It is up to you now to live it! It really is true that any good in us comes from Jesus Christ our Lord who is doing that godly activity that others recognize as being godly. The answer to the question, "How do we live by faith?" is simple. We are now and always to be completely dependent on God. Jesus said,

PART THREE — TO LIVE BY FAITH

"My righteous one shall live by faith." You are His righteous one. You and the rest of us shall live because of what Jesus is doing in us, and by what He is telling us to do.

Jesus faced temptation as He first started out in His ministry. You face temptation, too, and usually get hit the hardest when you begin thinking about living by faith. The Tempter (Satan) takes it very personally and points out various reasons to make you think what God has for you to do is impossible. We are faced with what seem to be impossible situations in life, and the enemy is quick to try to make us believe living by faith is, in itself, impossible. All of us who are surrendered to a life in Christ have experienced these temptations. If he fails to convince us, he then tries to show us how we will lose our friends and all that comforts us if we keep believing God. As followers of Jesus, we need to lose all the illusions of comfort that the world had given to us in the past. The world has nothing to offer us any more that is lasting or true. As the Tempter sees our mindset is death to old things and old ways, we show him, by our decisions that we no longer buy into those illusions.

> *We often overlook that Jesus was fully human. He had laid aside His privileges as God, and lived as a human. The risks He faced, we also face.*

We have begun a new adventuresome journey with God and are free from the bonds of the world. When we think this way, we are no longer subject to the enticements of the world and the temptations of Satan.

Jesus gives us this beautiful truth: *Are you weary and heavy-laden? Be yoked to Me. My yoke is easy and My burden is light. You will find rest for your souls!* Our soul is everything that makes us self-conscious. It refers to our self-awareness. Yoked to Jesus, we will find rest throughout our whole conscious self. Satan would deceive us so that we will remain in his darkness and absence of life rather than enter into God's light and eternal life. Jesus is not willing for us to remain Satan's captives. By faith, He releases us.

Part Three is a study of what living by faith looks like in a person's life. By faith, we live out what Jesus Christ gives us. It is focused and condensed for us in Hebrews 11 where different men and women of faith are cited in whose lives we might see how to live by faith. We must press forward into all that God has for us. Since this passage of Scripture is key to our understanding of faith, let us look again to Hebrews 11:1: "*Now faith is the assurance of things hoped for, the conviction of things not seen.*" Faith launches us forward, away from ourselves and into Jesus Christ's words and promises. The Bible is clear that "*faith comes from hearing, and hearing by the word of Christ*" (Romans 10:17). The more we understand Jesus' work, the more we understand the power of faith in our lives. Righteous living includes living by faith in Jesus' promises, Jesus' Words. When Hebrews 11:1 says, "*Now faith is,*" the verb is in a Greek form that means it is a continuous fact. Faith is our assurance that what God has promised he will fulfill, even in us. Our responsibility is to exercise faith in what God says!

First, living by faith is interrelated to our having assurance. We are assured of our faith because God said it. Faith believes God is, that He exists today as He always has, and that God

> *Living by faith is a greater adventure than any other adventure this world could ever offer.*

PART THREE — TO LIVE BY FAITH

does what He says. Faith believes that God's Word does not go forth from His mouth and return to Him void, but it shall accomplish all that God has set it out to do. (See Isaiah 55:11).

Assurance also means substance. Faith actually is the substance or material that forms or creates what we hope for concerning the Gospel. It has to do with salvation, new life and fellowship with God — all the Good News! A Word from God created all you see in the world around you. How many times did God say, "*Let there be...*" and there was? It is the same within our own lives. When God speaks into our lives, "*Let there be...*" then, you can be assured that it will be!

We see this in Jesus Christ's faith as he traveled this world as a human. We also see this understanding repeatedly in the men and women in the Bible. Remember, The Bible shows us only a few of the activities of Jesus to illustrate the numerous similar things He did as He lived among us. His daily routine was to be about the Father's business. Two times, we see Jesus multiply food. Several more times, He commands nature, and storms to cease and they do so at Jesus' command. Jesus raised the dead, healed the sick, gave sight to the blind, and healed withered limbs. Remember as we list Jesus' wonders that His faith was the same faith that we have available to us today. He is our example, the first in the inheritance that you and I also have with God. We are also sons and daughters of the Most High, as Jesus is the Firstborn Son. He had laid aside His privileges as God when He became a man (Philippians 2:7). The things Jesus did, He did with the same faith that He has given to us. He was the author of faith (Hebrews 12:2). He created it and lived it out first, then gave it to us. One may ask how does faith-material, that which we hope for, become visible material for believers like us? The answer is by our trust in God. We can see the result of such hope repeatedly demonstrated in the Bible. In the miracle of Jesus multiplying food, thousands were hungry and hoped for food. The lame hoped to walk; the blind hoped to see. The demon-possessed hoped for freedom. Those on life's stormy sea hope just as Peter hoped to be like our Lord. We hope, also, to walk above life's stormy sea. How many times has God answered our prayers and worked other miracles in us?

In these things, we see God's revelation and illustrations of the possibilities available to us as we hope and pray and live by faith. Verse one of Hebrews 11 ends at the new beginning of conviction that faith proves itself. It is *"The conviction of things not seen."* It is a fact that faith in your life is the conviction or evidence of the unseen Lord working in and through your life.

If we review the faith-forming teachings from the first ten chapters, almost all of those practices are evident in Hebrews 11. As God completes His work in us, and as the evidence of these things we hope for come to pass, our faith grows. We are then asked to step a bit higher and have faith for more. May God teach us to continually walk in faith and believe Him. One who stands still and never exercises faith is subject to live a stagnant life outside of God's potential. Read about the men and women of Hebrews and ask yourself, "Am I hoping against all hope like Abraham? Am I living by faith? ✝

CHAPTER

22

FAITH KNOWS TO DO RIGHT
Hebrews 11:4; Genesis 4:1–15

We are to live by faith as Abel lived by faith. "My righteousness one *shall* live by faith." This wonderful truth is an encouragement to us as it releases us by the understanding that our righteousness is not something we earn. It is a gift given to us by faith in Jesus Christ.

Faith results in a relationship with our Lord where He is our primary focus in life. As we look at the list of people in the Hall of Faith of Hebrews 11, we see Abel as our first illustration of a life lived by faith. *"By faith Abel offered to God a better sacrifice than Cain, through which he obtained the testimony that he was righteous, God testifying about his gifts, and through faith, though he is dead, he still speaks"* (Hebrews 11:4). That there could be a "better sacrifice" implies God had given previous worship instructions to Adam and Eve that were passed on to their children. That's how it can be said that Abel offered a better sacrifice than Cain. Cain didn't follow what he already knew to be the correct way to worship.

This event occurred after Adam and Eve were banned from the Garden of Eden. The Lord God did not abandon Adam and Eve at that time. Instead, their sin caused them to abandon their relationship with God. Adam and Eve changed, not God. God never left them, and He never leaves us. On their part, such change can be seen in their hiding from the Lord in shame. See Genesis 3:8. Having been changed by their sin, the Lord punished them. *"Therefore the Lord God sent him out from the Garden of Eden, to cultivate the ground from which he was taken. So He drove the man out; and at the east of the Garden of Eden He stationed the cherubim and the flaming sword which turned every direction to guard the way to the tree of life"* (Genesis 3:23-24).

It is both implied and stated that God, in His grace, gave them instructions for worship. Therefore we read, *"So it came about in the course of time that Cain brought an offering to the Lord of the fruit of the ground"* (Genesis 4:3). That phrase, *"in the course of time,"* speaks of a certain passing of time. Seemingly, this was not the first time the sons of Adam and Eve worshiped. God had instructed Adam and Eve concerning worship, and they passed it down to their children, including any other children after Cain and Abel. Other children born to Adam and Eve were not mentioned, for God's revelation is specific throughout the Bible. Here the Lord is marking the fork in the road of the growth of sin on one hand, as seen in Cain, and on the other hand, the growth of righteousness, as seen in Abel. Both Cain

22: FAITH KNOWS TO DO RIGHT

and Abel appear to be adults at this time. They may have been anywhere from twenty to a hundred years old or older, given the life expectancy of man in those times. Cain and Abel had been in the habit of worshiping for many years as their parents knew full well the dynamics of communing with God. Notice that the worship of both had been acceptable before this. Remember also that Jesus said we must not have anything against another before we come to worship, (Matthew 5:23-24). As we have all experienced, the tempter is always busy, whispering, prowling and disguised as our own thoughts. The Lord told Cain that sin was crouching, reaching for him at the door of his mind (Genesis 4:7). Child of God, notice in this verse that it says you can master the sin crouching at your door.

> *Often, we defend our desire to remain where we want to be rather than go where God wants us.*

Cain became resentful, and when a person allows resentment to enter, it spreads in his life. It festers and turns into rebellion against any authority. Cain directed his resentment toward his family and toward God. He then entered into his worship and God did not accept it. It happened this way: One day as they entered into worship, Cain brought an offering from his farm of vegetables and grain. This was probably his usual offering. Abel brought a first born from his flock. The word, *flock*, implies that his offering was a lamb. The Bible tells us the offering included even the fat portions of the lamb. Such an offering was the best of the best, a superior sacrifice. Both offerings could have been and would have been acceptable except that Cain's attitude, his heart, was not right with God. Offerings are to be given from the heart, with thanksgiving, reverence, and with care. Abel's offering was acceptable. Cain's was not. Many have not fully understood God's reasoning in this. As you can see here, the rejection did not have as much to do with the physical offering as with the condition of the heart of the person making the offering. The condition of our hearts is what is most important to God. Cain was angry at God's rejection, and the anger revealed that his heart was not right as he gave his sacrifice. A person who respects the Lord and wants to please Him may conceivably be angry about their offering being rejected, but would then search to see what they had done wrong that would cause God to reject their offering. That person would want to know what they did wrong so they could change their ways in order to please God. Cain did not humble himself to see his own wrongdoing. His focus was on himself rather than on pleasing God. He was stubborn and rebellious. His countenance fell and revealed his heart. In this case, the falling was into the hands of another, the Tempter.

Immediately, the Lord addressed Cain's anger and his fallen countenance explaining to him that if he did well, he would be accepted. God offered Cain an opportunity to reverse his attitude and repent. Cain continued doing wrong even after this opportunity was presented by God. Notice the grace of God, and how the Lord offered him a way out. He said, *"If you do well, will not your countenance be lifted up?* Sin had ensnared him. We must be careful to listen for the opportunities where God is leading us to the same areas of repentance. Are you resentful for someone else's success? Can we not improve ourselves in the eyes of the Lord and not get

22: FAITH KNOWS TO DO RIGHT

mired down in jealousy and bitterness? In the next verse, Genesis 4:8, we read, "*Cain told Abel his brother.*" The verb "*told*" is a strong word. It is interpreted as "*said*" in Genesis chapter one, and is the Hebrew word used eight times when God spoke the world into existence. It shows the great authority of God and His creative power. The word is also used in Psalm 94:4-7, where the Psalmist writes: "*They pour out their arrogant words; all the evildoers boast. They crush your people, O Lord, and afflict your heritage. They kill the widow and the sojourner, and murder the fatherless; and they say, 'The Lord does not see...'*"(ESV).

Cain must have been strongly defending the case of his rebellion against God before Abel, using strong words to impress Abel. Luke 11:50-51 tells us Abel was a prophet. There is, then, a strong possibility that the Lord gave Abel redemptive words to speak to Cain concerning his stubborn, prideful behavior. If Abel had spoken a prophetic word to Cain, then Cain was probably strongly defending his position against Abel's prophetic words rather than repenting and finding forgiveness and reconciliation. Often, we defend our desire to remain where we want to be rather than go where God wants us. Then, we invariably become offended at those trying to help us.

Later, in the field, Cain murdered Abel. He would rather murder his brother than receive God's words. In this story about Cain and Abel, we see that evil was spreading quickly in that pre-flood culture. Abel was doing his part to contain it, and to spread righteousness. His heart, the person he was in the center of his being, was right before God. How does a righteous person live? Righteous people are humble enough to let God change how they think, what they do, and where they go.

DOORWAYS to Greater Faith

They respond positively to what God says, accepting and learning from correction, and follow His direction. They obey God. They speak out in favor of God. They yearn for God's way. They give God their best. In effect, they let God continue His work through them. As Abel believed, Abel acted. He lived by faith.☦

STUDY QUESTIONS:

1. What new conclusion for your life have you discovered about living by faith? What differences do you see between Cain and Abel? Why did these differences matter to God?
2. How have you changed inside because of your faith? Have you heard God speak to you about some habit or behavior displeasing to Him?
3. In what ways do you seek to help your brothers and sisters in Christ? Do you pray for them?
4. In what ways does sin separate us from God? How is that gap closed?
5. What are some changes that you know will help you grow in faith? Do you handle your differences with your brothers and sisters in Christ with redeeming love?

CHAPTER 23

FAITH THAT LIVES FOREVER
Genesis 5:21–24; Hebrews 11:5–6

Enoch was a man of God who never died. His name means, *"initiated"* or *"disciplined,"* and it carries a message for us. A person of faith disciplines their life by a deliberate arrangement of their priorities and interests. Faith is a commitment to God where what was once important to us becomes less important because of God's presence in our lives. Such faith causes a person to realize that they have higher purposes than the worldly purposes once held. Faith focuses us on what God wants. We still have our earthly lives to live, just as Jesus did. We still have relationships, needs, and cares in this world as Jesus had. However, we have a new focus and a new direction in our lives

We are never too young or too old to walk with God or for God to fulfill whatever desires He puts in our hearts.

DOORWAYS to Greater Faith

now. God has renewed our minds and softened our hearts toward Him. He has given us His Spirit. The Bible says we are new beings, that we have a new character. We were created to walk with God, forever!

Enoch was the son of Jared. See Luke 3:37. In Biblical history, the name *"Jared"* was thought to mean a sign of the degeneration of the human race. Therefore, it was a special thing that in a culture rapidly falling away from God, Enoch stood out as one who chose to walk with God. It is no doubt that this life focus was as difficult for him as it is for us today. It was not a simple culture or a simple time. There were many demands and much confusion about the things of God. Man, without God, loves himself most. Enoch was special in God's eyes and became a special part of the culture of his day. We are to be special to God and make a difference in our own world.   In Jude, verses 14-16, referring to the evilness of the culture in which Enoch lived, we read, *"It was also about these men that Enoch, in the seventh generation from Adam, prophesied, saying, 'behold, the Lord came with many thousands of His holy ones, to execute judgment upon all, and to convict all the ungodly of all their ungodly deeds which they have done in an ungodly way, and of all the harsh things which ungodly sinners have spoken against Him.' These are grumblers, finding fault, following after their own lusts; they speak arrogantly, flattering people for the sake of gaining an advantage."* Well, that's enough of today's news, but, believe it or not, these verses were about the condition of people's hearts in the days of Enoch — several thousand years ago!

Enoch's relationship with God set him at odds with his culture. Enoch was not quiet about his walk with God. Jude tells

23: FAITH THAT LIVES FOREVER

us he was a prophet, so he was prophesying and teaching the people. He was a man of honor, had the high principles of God in his life, and no doubt held the principles of God before his culture. He was a very overt man of God. Each day of his life, he must have practiced much of what we studied of the building blocks we learned in Jesus' School of Faith-Forming. He was not intimidated by the world's ways or anyone in the world. He knew and also practiced the authority of God. He was submitted to a life following the will of God. Enoch reached out and touched God's heart daily. He guarded his own thoughts and words. He was a persistent man and his goal was to see his own people brought back to God.

He walked with Almighty God. At age sixty-five Enoch had his son, Methuselah. Nothing is impossible with God. We are never too young or too old to walk with God or for God to fulfill whatever desires He puts in our hearts. At his age, after the birth of his son, we are told Enoch walked with God for three hundred more years. Then one day, he walked on into heaven with God, at age three hundred and sixty five. The Bible says, *"he was not"* in Genesis 5:24. The word, *"not,"* means he no longer existed on this earth. There was no body found, no grave needed for burial. He went straight to heaven without dying.

Enoch's relationship with God was such that they strolled along together like Adam and God did in the beginning, full of peace, sharing their love and friendship closely. One day during one of their walks, I can imagine Enoch, feeling light on his feet, looking down and discovering he was walking on air, going higher and higher. God really does love us so much that He wants constant and familiar fellowship, just like Adam and God, like Enoch and God — you and God. This is what walking by faith looks like.

Let's investigate this event in Enoch's life a bit more. To walk with God means more than just a constant realization of God's presence, or our continuous efforts at obedience. To walk with God implies a most confidential intimacy with the personal God, a Father/son or daughter relationship. It implies a nearness to God, continual communion with Him where we talk and listen to His voice, and He does the same with us. Such an intimacy is not burdened with feelings of personal unworthiness. Such an intimacy is our being highly aware that God has done all that is needed for us to live full lives, and we have accepted what He has done. We can walk with Him in complete joy as He is our strength and our reason for being.

I'm reminded of Proverbs 4:18: *"The path of the righteous is like the light of dawn, that shines brighter and brighter until the full day."* Enoch strikes me as being a man who was focused on God and on the future. Too often we focus on the experiences we had yesterday or the troubles we are enduring today. Enoch wasn't focused on the past. One's past cannot be changed. He was focused on God, and God was pleased with him. His relationship with God did not waver. He understood what it meant to walk with God as Adam had in the garden. Enoch was steadfast and full of wisdom, and God pulled him forward and right on into heaven. Enoch had made it through this life, by the grace of God. He was so into the Lord God that there was no longer anything for him here. Was it that he

23: FAITH THAT LIVES FOREVER

reached a point of such focus that leaving God was impossible? We don't know the exact reason. We do know that all things are possible with God. We know Enoch existed on this earth one moment and the next he was gone to be with God. We also know Jesus said all things are possible for us, too. When we become so caught up in God that our lives are all about doing God's will, our will is lost in Him. On his walk with God, Enoch's life style with God was such that he walked right on home to be with His Father.

Enoch is one of only two humans who never died on earth. Elijah was the other. Enoch's life and name represents something worthy of taking note. As already mentioned, his name means, *"initiated"* or *"disciplined."* One undergoes initiation when he or she is given admittance into a particular society, such as God's eternal kingdom. To be *"disciplined"* is to have the character of faith needed to reach that new society. The person who is living under a specific discipline chooses the discipline. It is not a discipline imposed by someone else as is often done in churches. Disciples are disciplined followers of Jesus.

All of the lives of the faithful represent something. We are clearly taught in Hebrews 10:38 and 11:5-6 that Enoch's life represents a life lived by faith. Such a life is of monumental note. It is actually miraculous, too, for it is a gift from God. Remember that as you live your life under God's discipline. It is a miracle in you, too. We obey God, but we do it because we love Him and walk with Him. We do not obey in our own power, but in God's power as we discipline ourselves to obey by faith. When Jesus says such things as, *"follow Me,"* or *"he who follows will not walk in darkness,"* or *"abide in Me,"* we are getting the same call as Enoch. To abide in Jesus Christ means to remain in His presence. It means to be one with Him in mind, heart, and spirit. It also refers to steadfastness and to persevering.

Jesus said, *"If you continue in My word, then you are truly disciples of Mine; and you will know the truth, and the truth will make you free"* (John 8:31–32).

"My righteous one shall live by faith." Righteous persons arrange their priorities and discipline themselves so their lives will be increasingly open to God. Living by faith is a commitment to those things that are important to God, not to things that are important to us. The desire in our hearts is to do the will of God. It results in a reaching for and a touching of the heart of God. We, in turn, will then live peaceful, joy-filled, abundant lives with those around us. We will shine brighter and brighter with each step we take closer to God, until the full day.

We spoke of revolutionary faith in an earlier chapter. This kind of walk and faith is revolutionary to this world. In Enoch's time, his walk with God was revolutionary. It is God's desire that we walk the same way. What wonderful examples God gives us of walking in revolutionary faith. ☨

STUDY QUESTIONS:

1. In what ways did Enoch live that you feel you should be living today?
2. Have you felt Enoch's kind of closeness to God? Do you walk with God? Do you want to walk with God?

23: FAITH THAT LIVES FOREVER

3. Has your walk with God ever been noticed by those looking on? Are you a light to others? As this is so, remember to thank God because such a life in you is a gift from Him.
4. Do you sense that God is using you to touch others whether you say a word or not? When this is so, God's Spirit is at work in you.
5. Do you note and accept the miraculous activity of God in your life? Do you think this is for others and not for you? If so, why?

CHAPTER 24

ᚠAITH THAT ᚱEQUIRES ᛖXTRAORDINARY ᛟBEDIENCE
Genesis 6:11–22; Hebrews 11:7

Living by faith is such a priority for the believer that God reaches back to the beginning of mankind to show us how it is done. We see this pattern begin to appear in a man who God sought, and his name was Noah.

We quickly learn here that nothing we might experience can interfere with or is beyond what God may call us to do. Just as God saw Noah's faith and called on him to respond beyond his experience, God also calls on us in our day. For instance, our Bible reading in Genesis and Hebrews as stated above, says that God warned Noah about things not yet seen. God's righteous people are called to move on into anything God might require, even those things some may have not yet

> *We have come to times when radical and revolutionary faith like that of Noah's is urgent.*

24: FAITH THAT REQUIRES EXTRAORDINARY OBEDIENCE

seen; things like our reigning in life, like us imitating Christ, or like us having the right or authority to become children of God in our faith life (John 1:12). God talks to us as we are His children. Just like earthly parents speak with and expect their own children to listen, we, too, are called by our Heavenly Father to listen and adhere to His voice.

Jesus said, *"My sheep hear My voice, and I know them, and they follow Me"* (John 10:27). This is what Noah did. Noah heard God's voice. How does one hear the voice of God? There are many ways that God speaks to a believer. Sometimes His voice is similar to a feeling that He is there and wants you to do a certain thing. At other times, it is as if words are spoken and the will of God forms in a person's own thoughts. This is the Holy Spirit bearing witness with our own spirit concerning what God wants us to do. At other times, thoughts or directions may rise up within us while we are reading the Bible and God's will is made known to us. There are different ways that God communicates. We discussed dreams in an earlier chapter. God says His Creation reveals God's eternal power and divine nature. Creation testifies to the existence and knowledge of God (See Romans 1:20,21). God said we hear Him. God promises that we, as His sheep, would hear Him and know His voice. We can believe God in this. Nothing is impossible for Him.

The refreshing thing about John 10:27 is that, as God's sheep, we can also discern His voice from the other voices around and within us. God promised the Holy Spirit would lead us and guide our lives by the use of peace. In John 16:33 Jesus said, *"These things I have spoken to you, so that in Me you may have peace."* When God speaks to us, His words heard in our conscience or spirit bring us peace. Many of Paul's letters are introduced with the phrase: *"Grace to you and peace from God our Father and the Lord Jesus Christ."* That is, God was about to communicate through that letter to those who read that letter. It is a valid understanding that when you hear God speak to you it will bring peace.

God spoke to Noah telling him to build an ark. He told Noah it was going to rain, to rain enough to flood the world. As the water came both from above and from below, the interesting thing for Noah is that, in his time, the Bible teaches it had not rained on the earth as yet. The earth had been watered with a mist prior to this. (Genesis 2:6). Moses had never seen rain. He had no idea of what an ark was or the possible use of it. God asked Noah to perform an outrageous, and to the world around him, an illogical act.

God asked Noah to believe that completely and totally illogical things were about to happen. Noah was walking in a bold faith the likes of which we are called to experience. Yes! The days are here for us.

God is calling us to this kind of faith. Now is the time! We have come to times when radical and revolutionary faith like that of Noah's is urgent. It is urgent for the saving of our lives and those whom we are called to make disciples of in all the nations (Matthew 28:19). We must listen and obey God regarding these things. We have the advantage of learning by others' experiences, including those in Hebrews Chapter Eleven Hall of Faith. God instructed Noah concerning things that didn't yet exist and could hardly be imagined by that culture. Noah built that ark, nonetheless.

24: FAITH THAT REQUIRES EXTRAORDINARY OBEDIENCE

That pre-flood culture numbered as many humans in existence as our culture has today. People lived much longer during this time period. Start with Adam and Eve, and then began multiplying. If we consider all those mentioned in the Bible before the flood and multiply it out, figuring each family had three sons and three daughters, we can consider their inhabitants had to be as numerous as our population today. It was a flourishing culture. They had metal works, building projects, art, cultivation, records were actively maintained. Religions, and many other areas of development were in progress. God said, about that culture, that every intention of their thoughts was slanted toward evil. (See Genesis 6:5). That is, mankind's every purpose and plan was evil, selfish and harmful, except for that of one man, Noah.

Think of how easily we can be overwhelmed by the evil we see around us in our time. Without faith, we would feel hopeless and helpless at times. Noah did not become overwhelmed by the behavior he saw around him. He continued to walk in faith. He never became intimidated by the mockery of his neighbors as they passed by and saw him working on a beast of a project of which they had no concept. Imagine again being asked by God to do something so grandiose that it was impossible to hide. There was no hiding of this task from the sneering onlookers. He could not hide out in his basement, so Noah decided to be bold about it all and proceed without allowing anyone to delay him. He was a prophet. As God had spoken to him regarding what was to come, Noah also knew that time was of the essence. In Genesis 9:25–27, Noah spoke a curse that was aimed at Ham's son, Canaan's descendants, and a blessing was upon the descendants of his sons Shem and Japeth. This prophecy by Noah, Bible scholars say, laid the foundation for Israel's future foreign policy. God was about the business of speaking with Noah and Noah listened and tried to help others as he was a preacher of righteousness. II Peter 2:5 says: *"(God) preserved Noah, a preacher of righteousness, with seven others, when He brought a flood upon the world of the ungodly."* Noah didn't just listen to the catcalls of those passing, He preached to them about sin and righteousness, and prophesied about the coming flood and called the people to repent. He wasn't overwhelmed either by his job or by those rejecting him. He was focused on God's will, not his feelings or a need for popularity. He was extraordinarily obedient. Four times we read in Genesis that Noah did all that God commanded him to do. *"Thus Noah did; according to all that God had commanded him, so he did"* (Genesis 6:22). Similar statements are also found in Genesis 7:5; 7:9; and 7:16.

Be encouraged by this man who lived by faith in his generation. God is straightforward with us and gives direction to those who will listen and live by faith today. He presents His saints to us clearly. He speaks of both their sin and of their faithfulness to encourage us that, even in our human weakness we, too, can also live with an extraordinary faith. He revealed that Noah was as fallible as we are. Noah got drunk when the flood was over and did some very strange things that were out of line with God (Genesis 9:21). However, it does seem to have a prophetic leaning. After all, we know that Isaiah went naked and barefoot for three years in his prophetic ministry (Isaiah 20:3).

24: FAITH THAT REQUIRES EXTRAORDINARY OBEDIENCE

We also know that God's Word says any believer can and will live by faith: "*My righteous one shall live by faith.*" The word, "*shall,*" is in a Greek form here that means you will take upon yourself the purpose of living by faith. It is spoken of as a fact. The responsibility of living by faith is yours, and as you love God you will live by faith.

Noah turned his life over to the doing of God's will. That is an illustration of the righteous living by faith. To live by faith is a deliberate choice one makes. God does not force His will upon us. Rather, we reach a point in our relationship with God where pleasing Him becomes more important to us than to live the way we were living before. We become a part of God's plan. We become all that God created us to be.

Noah chose God's will, God's way, and God's purpose, and saved his family. God used Noah's family to raise up a new, post flood culture. Through the generation of Shem, Noah's son, God's chosen people are founded, and through his descendants Jesus Christ is born. Noah walked by faith and was used by God. God still has a plan and, as long as this world exists, He has a plan for each generation. Let God call you into His kind of faith. When you opened your heart to Jesus Christ, God reached into your heart (Hebrews 8:10), performed spiritual heart surgery and made you a new creature. We are fully equipped to exercise extraordinary faith and obedience. We have been transformed. Our hearts are made new and desire to do God's will and live by faith!✝

DOORWAYS to Greater Faith

STUDY QUESTIONS:

1. Is God so real and so close in your life that you feel bold to speak out about Him?
2. Noah was not influenced at all by a world with a culture similar to ours . He cared for God and he cared for the people; so he obeyed God without question. What does that speak into your life? Is God asking you to do something that is outside your comfort level?
3. Noah preached righteousness and prophesied and not one person responded. Do you allow it to hinder your walk with God when you speak to others about how they need God and they ignore you or mock you? Do you continue to pray for them?
4. What do you feel needs to be changed in your life in order to live by faith?
5. The Bible speaks of there being times to proclaim a thing. Do you feel such a moving in your life, that it is time to proclaim to yourself and to your Lord that the time is here to move forward in a style of living that calls for extraordinary faith?

CHAPTER 25

FAITH THAT AFFECTS ALL GENERATIONS
Hebrews 11:8-10, 17-19

There is a tendency to think people like Abraham, Moses, David, Mary, and Paul had a call from God and a faith to match that overshadows any call and faith that we could possibly have today. For instance, Abraham was called to be the father of a nation through which God would reveal Himself. Moses was called to free God's people from Pharaoh and lead them to the Promised Land. David was called to be the king of God's people in the Promised Land. Mary was called to be a virgin mother through whom the Son of God, Jesus Christ, would be born among us. Paul was called to bear Jesus' Name before the Gentiles and kings as well as before the sons of Israel to preach the good news that Jesus Christ had come to reconcile man to God. These people were called to unique positions to do unique things. Notice that there is a common thread in their purpose toward God's master plan that He has spelled out for us in His Word. Each person began a purpose that was continued by the next toward God's redemption of mankind. God is doing the same with us today. Until Jesus Christ returns, God's plan will endure to His final redemption. The same as the lives of these men and women of the Bible affected each other and future generations, our lives and purpose in God will affect others and future generations as well.

We are men and women with God's Spirit living in us. We are called into a new life, an Enoch type, personal and intimate walk with God. We are called to revolutionary faith in being obedient to the call on our lives by God, like Noah. God also calls us to give ourselves to Him like Abraham for the benefit of others and for those who will follow us. As we walk in this new life, in the purpose God created us to fulfill, we tell others what Jesus has done and is doing in our lives. This also entices others to pray and find God's purpose for them.

There are many special callings and positions God calls us into: Pastors, teachers, prophets, evangelists and apostles. We are to reflect Jesus in whatever position God calls us to serve. Each person who has faith in Jesus Christ is important and is called to do what God asks. One call Jesus has given to all believers is to make disciples of all the nations and to teach them to obey all that He commanded us (Matthew 28:19-20). You can be sure God will speak to you. Just as He gives examples in His Word, He will reveal your purpose to you as He revealed His purpose to those who are willing to follow Him.

25: FAITH THAT AFFECTS ALL GENERATIONS

As we discussed a bit before, a disciple is a person, whom we call a Christian or a believer in Jesus, who is to become attached to Jesus and to follow Him in His teachings. This person has submitted to Jesus and recognizes he or she is called to the disciple's way of life. Each call God places on such a life is as unique as Abraham's call because we all have unique circumstances in which to serve, unique people to reach and a unique time in history to serve Him.

As we proceed, remember that people mentioned in Scripture are shown as examples to reveal the ways that God calls and works and fellowships with each of us, even and especially *you*! We are to follow Jesus as a body of believers where we realize the importance of each individual who makes up the Body of Christ. As you are surrendered to a life in Christ, that means you are a part of the Body and are called!

Abraham is God's example of a man of faith for us. Abraham's faith life began at the call of God, and Abraham's call came before he knew much about God. He learned more about God as he walked with Him in faithfulness. God called Abraham to leave his home and start out in search of the land he was promised by God. He didn't even know where he was going (Hebrews 11:8), and hadn't had the experience yet of following God. Each of us needs to get hold of this for our lives! After initially finding faith in Christ, we are already out of the gate and into the race. Through faith Abraham, when called, placed all of his future in God's hands. As we read, Abraham made

> *...we all have unique circumstances in which to serve, unique people to reach and a unique time in history to serve Him.*

mistakes at times, but God lovingly corrects him and Abraham turns around each time with a refreshed commitment. It is better to make occasional mistakes serving God than never to move forward and step out in faith. As Abraham focused his life and direction toward God's will, we are to do the same. *"Let us lay aside every encumbrance and the sin which so easily entangles us, and let us run with endurance the race that is set before us"* (Hebrews 12:1).

We know that, most of the time, we fall too easily into the trap of reason. We sacrifice faith in order to impress others with the wonder of our own knowledge and wisdom. We seem to forget that our concern is not to be about us, but about Jesus and about others. Jesus is truly the answer to our questions about faith and the problems we encounter in life. We do not look to Jesus enough. We must be like Abraham and leap into a faith-filled life with God with the innocence of a young child who leaps into his father's arms. We are to do this while knowing and expecting to be cradled and loved. Jesus said God wants us to come to Him as little children. With all that God has in store for our lives, we truly can be excited, expectant and impressionable about the things our Father has planned for us.

Consider Abraham's leap of faith. God told Abraham and Sarah that they were going to have a child. They waited and, yes, worried for twenty-five years. They even tried to force God's hand after they had waited fifteen years (Gen 16:2). God never changed His plan for them: Abraham and *Sarah* were going to have that special child through whose genealogy the Messiah would come. This was *not* going to happen through

25: FAITH THAT AFFECTS ALL GENERATIONS

Abraham and Sarah's maid, Hagar and her subsequent son, Ishmael. God fulfilled His promise to Abraham and Sarah. Isaac was born. Later, when God tested Abraham's faith, for God repeatedly tests our faith as we all soon find out, Abraham was going to obey God even if it meant sacrificing Isaac. Remember, Isaac is the son God promised. Abraham was willing to keep believing. God had said He was going to build a great nation through Abraham's descendants — through Isaac. Isaac had to live! Abraham thought that through as he went up the mountain with Isaac to offer him to God. The Bible tells us that Abraham came to the worldly impossible understanding that *"God is able to raise people even from the dead"* (Hebrews 11:19). Abraham believed that God could raise Isaac from the dead. If that is what God had to do in order to fulfill the promise that Abraham believed God for, Abraham knew God would do it! Do we believe God that way about the vision He has given us? The Lord stopped Abraham from sacrificing Isaac when He saw Abraham's willingness to obey, when He saw Abraham's willingness to give back to God his long desired son, Isaac.

Faith is always a leap into the unknown. In such leaps, a person moves forward, by faith, into the Lord's will. In our faith trials, Jesus doesn't want us to go back where we once were when He called us forward. He wants us to move into where we have not yet been. When God said, *"My righteous one shall live by faith,"* He means for you to move into startling wonders and seemingly impossible situations. As we spend personal time with God, He reveals those things He wants us to do and places He wants us to go. That is your vision — your Promised Land!

DOORWAYS to Greater Faith

In our generation, each believer is being called into a refreshing experience of his or her faith. There is a tendency today to raise our voices and argue against faith, against stepping into the unknown, against what God promises. In our pride, we believe we know more than God, who has already revealed what we need to know in Jesus Christ. We need to remember that we are the ones who serve God and not the other way around. Paul said, *"See to it that no one takes you captive through philosophy and empty deception, according to the tradition of men, according to the elementary principles of the world, rather than according to Christ"* (Colossians 2:8). Again, as always, living by faith is being more Christ-conscious in the many different moments of our lives. We also see that living by faith is believing that God is always right, and will always fulfill what He says, even if we have to leave behind things we once thought were wonderfully wise. What is good is not always God's best for us. God's righteous people are those who believe what God promises or says. Romans 4:21-22 reveals to us that God credits such faith as righteousness. We are to live by faith in Jesus Christ. Abraham did that by obeying God. His obedience carried out a new way of life that has spread from generation to generation of a people called after God's own name. What a wonderful thing! Abraham's faith began and ours takes off where his leaves off. We are heirs of Abraham, too! We, too, are God's chosen people, those who have surrendered our lives to His will, those who choose to live in faith. It is exciting to know how far reaching simple acts of faith can ripple through history. Several thousands of years have passed and God is still the same and He is calling you!☦

25: FAITH THAT AFFECTS ALL GENERATIONS

STUDY QUESTIONS:

1. What do you think of your calling to live like a son or daughter of God? Will you?
2. What is Jesus doing in your life right now?
3. What are some of the ways God has tested your faith?
4. Has God given you something and asked you to give it back?
5. How do you feel about faith leading you to move on into what is yet unknown? Remember that it is not faith if it is known or if you already have all the answers.
6. What effect does obedience have on faith? How are you working this out in your life?
7. Have you been prompted to speak to someone out of the clear blue and followed through with surprising results?

CHAPTER

26

𝐿IVING BY 𝐹AITH
Various Scriptures

𝒲ithout faith it is impossible to please God. He who comes to God must believe that He is, and that He rewards those who seek Him (Hebrews 11:6). God speaks of *"living by faith"* in Him as the most pleasing attitude a human can have toward God. He tells that it is a good testimony, an action of which He approves. *"For by it, the men of old gained approval"* (Hebrews 11:2). We live in a world with severe problems. It is a world full of sin and God is calling us to separate ourselves from it. The only way we can do that is to return to Him by faith and look to Him in what He will do to solve the sin problem.

When Adam and Eve sinned by eating of the fruit of the Tree of Knowledge of Good and Evil, at that moment they became aware of themselves. They saw their nakedness. Before

26: LIVING BY FAITH

succumbing to temptation, they lived in a state of innocence and trust in God. They walked with God in the Garden, experienced His fellowship and approval. God wants to walk with us and have us experience His fellowship and approval. What must walking in such innocence have been like? Adam and Eve surely saw and appreciated the difference in themselves. They were made for each other, to complement each other in every way. They surely were not blind to the wonder of love and each other. They had better vision than we have, being unhampered by generations of gene pool mixture.

Before Eve was created, Adam had the Garden of Eden to cultivate and keep (Genesis 2:15). When Eve was created she joined with Adam in his work. This is where the serpent found them, in the garden together, cultivation and keeping it. They were conscious of themselves and, I am sure they were enjoying the beauty of life. Mostly, they were conscious of God. They knew their personal needs, and being without clothing did not even enter their consciousness. Surely, the existence God had given them included His gift of a sexual and intimate relationship. God's creation was perfect and it included the command, "*Be fruitful and multiply*" (Genesis 1:28). Apparently, before sin their conscious life reached out to God primarily. Then, secondarily they reached out to meet each other's needs. However, God was their glory. What an example this is for married folk today! God was their prime focus.

Their normal activity was to be aware of God. To see anything else, they had to choose to look away from God. Now think of how this is opposite to our thinking process today. We have to look away from ourselves to see God. For Adam and

Eve, this was about to end. What must such a life have been like? I believe we can see an example of that in Jesus Christ. When Jesus walked this earth as fully human, we must always remind ourselves that in all accounts of His life in Matthew, Mark, Luke, and John, He had laid aside His privileges as God and lived a human life just like us, minus sin. Scripture says, "*Although He existed in the form of God,* (Jesus) *did not regard equality with God a thing to be grasped, but emptied Himself, taking the form of a bond-servant* (a human)" (Philippians 2:6-7, in parentheses mine).

Jesus' attitude toward living a truly human life is revealed in His prayer to the Father: "*All things that are Mine are Yours*" (John 17:10). This life, like the one Jesus lived, is the kind of life Adam and Eve enjoyed before they sinned. They were God's property. Quite simply, the same as a human baby, God provided all that Adam and Eve needed. Just as a baby trusts an adult to care for it, knowing nothing different, we are to have the same kind of faith in God as a new creation in Him. Adam and Eve knew that kind of trust and faith, and Jesus died so that we could have it back.

We will learn to listen for God's voice more and more each time we step out in faith to do what He speaks in our spirit.

When Adam and Eve sinned, the purity and innocence of God's truth no longer resided in them. A mental shift occurred in them when they sinned, and it was the death of their innocence and the innocence of mankind. Adam and Eve had rebelled against God. Rebellion became a natural event in their thought life and in their actions. The self-centered nature of Sa-

26: LIVING BY FAITH

tan was born in mankind. Before, God was first and everything else to Adam and Eve was second. When they reached out in rebellion, to be like God, it turned the world upside down. Reality and truth were turned upside down. Satan is good at doing this to us. Therefore, faith is that gift of God that enables us to return to the focus — the same attitude Adam and Eve started with, *"All that I have is Yours, Lord."*

We see more of Jesus' example of living by faith in the book of John, which was written to give us a wider view of these truths,. Jesus said all things that are His are God's which includes all of Jesus' living activities. So we read, *"Truly, truly, I say to you (to us), the Son can do nothing of Himself, unless it is something He sees the Father doing; for whatever the Father does, these things the Son also does in like manner. For the Father loves the Son, and shows Him all things that He Himself is doing; and the Father will show Him greater works than these, so that you will marvel"* (John 5:19-20). *"I do not seek My own will, but the will of Him who sent Me"* (John 5:30). *"I do nothing on My own initiative, but I speak these things as the Father taught Me"* (John 8:28). As we have discussed before, the Father always took the leading step in what Jesus did or said. As a man, Jesus lived by faith. All of His rights and thoughts and actions and purposes were that of the Father's.

Jesus said His sheep hear His voice. At times, in every believer, we become aware of conversations occurring in our minds. Thoughts about people or situations surface in such a way that we know we have received instructions to do a certain thing. The instructions might be very simple, such as to speak a happy "hello" to someone, or we might hear more complex instructions. God talks to some when they are needy, to others when He has a particular plan for them to fulfill. You have read of such things in the Bible. God is still the same. At these times, we realize that we are hearing the voice of our God as He directs us to do certain things. For strange reasons we often ignore these instructions. It is either because of ignorance or disobedience. I have sometimes been obedient to such instructions from God. If we are obedient, it will cause an awakening in us. We will learn to listen for God's voice more and more each time we step out in faith to do what He speaks in our spirit. We need to learn to recognize when our instructions are from God and when they come from Satan. Such voice recognition is easier than we think at first. For instance, God's words are redemptive, loving, comforting, encouraging, freeing, and meet needs. In other words, they are like the words Jesus spoke to people. In contrast, Satan's words are also contradictory to what God has said in the Bible. For instance, Satan urges us to put ourselves at the center of our life and work. He urges self-centeredness and self reliance. We learn to hear and discern God's voice the more we walk with Him.

God is calling us, and He yearns for us to walk with Him in such a way that our daily moment-by-moment life will be His. The life of Adam and Eve, as they walked with God in the Garden in the cool of the day is the kind of walk that God wants to have with you! The enemy tries to make us think this could never be possible. He tries to cause us to fear such a life, but Jesus tells us repeatedly, to *"fear not."* When the angel was about to tell Mary that God had chosen to use her to give birth

26: LIVING BY FAITH

to His Son, the angel said, *"fear not"* (Luke 1:30). When Peter was about to be called to be a disciple after Jesus had miraculously given him a catch of fish, Jesus comforted him by telling him to fear not. (Luke 5:10). Satan would like to prevent Jesus' plans, and therefore tries to arouse fear in us. Repeatedly, Jesus directs us to trust Him in our circumstances, and to fear not. If God is for us, who can be against us?

We read what Abel did by faith and so, too, about Enoch and Noah and Abraham and Sarah. Then, in Hebrews 11:32, we read of numerous others who performed acts of righteousness, obtained promises, quenched the power of fire, resurrected the dead, healed people and lived great lives of faith in the Name of Jesus and walked without fear. They may have had fear when they began, but as they stepped out in faith beyond their fear, God rewarded their faithfulness.

God approved of their faith. They were looking to a future that God had promised, a celestial city and eternity with God. Their faith changed their lives and the lives of others around them and still changes lives today.

Because of the life of Jesus, we know there are yet heights of faith that we can reach, and those heights are found in listening to the voice of the Holy Spirit as we follow in the footsteps of Jesus. Jesus told us that He could not stay here on this earthly plane because He needed to send back God's promise, the Holy Spirit, to empower us to do the will of God in the same way that the Holy Spirit empowered Him (See Romans 8:11). As I have researched this topic of faith, and while writing this book, I have become increasingly sure that the Lord is calling each of us forward into a life full of faith in Him. God calls us into an increasing awareness of who Jesus Christ is to us, our way to do all things for God, our way to God! He is our Savior, our Brother, and our Friend.

Paul urges, *"It is already the hour for you to awaken from sleep"* (Romans 13:11); *"Awake, sleeper, and arise from the dead, and Christ will shine on you"* (Ephesians 5:14). Let us awaken from our sleep and answer this call to the fullness of life we have been called to live. Let us be captivated by the presence of God in our lives and live only to serve Him and others! We can do all things through Christ who strengthens us! (See Philippians 4:13). Let us live this life where we become so captivated with Him that He increasingly becomes the prime mover in our lives. The door of faith and opportunity is open to us. Jesus says, *"Follow Me!"* ‡

Study Questions:

1. Have you given yourself reasons to go further in your relationship with Jesus Christ? In what ways is the enemy causing you to fear obeying God?
2. What do you recognize as the source of your reason?
3. What is your primary focus in life? Are you like Adam and Eve before the fall, spending time alone with God and loving on Him?
4. What are some of the things you have heard God speak to you? Are you familiar with His voice? Can you discern the difference between God's voice, the enemy's voice and your own voice?
5. Right now, what do your believe Jesus is calling you to do?

CHAPTER 27

CALLED INTO A LIFE BY FAITH
Various Scriptures

Faith grows. In Part One of this book we studied ten teachings of Jesus about faith. Each teaching was a deeper look into faith. We looked at Jesus' teaching as a school in which Jesus was forming the faith of His followers. Jesus encouraged them to move forward in their faith. Each teaching focused and refocused more deeply on Jesus Christ. We did not focus primarily on our own actions lest we mistakenly think that growing in faith is something we do rather than understand that it is a gift of God.

As faith continues to grow, we then studied some of the facets of faith; how they are similar to a diamond. Through each facet, we can see the full beauty and spiritual richness of this gift from God. We look up to God and look back into history to see the acts of Jesus and others as they moved on into the depths of faith. God intends for us to see and learn. We

DOORWAYS to Greater Faith

have seen how faith transforms people, and how God honors them. We saw the risks involved in stepping out in faith. Then, we saw faith's influence in the deepest parts of our lives, in our minds and our hearts. We saw how it reaches on into the future.

We have learned what God meant when He said the righteous, or just, shall live by faith. When people live by faith, their assurance in God's promises continually increases. Then faith, as a spiritual reality or material, grows in them.

Since faith does continue to grow, no one has yet experienced the fullest meaning of it. For instance, toward the end of his life, Paul spoke of pressing on toward the goal for the prize of the upward call of God in Christ Jesus. (See Philippians 3:14). In His absolute humanity, Jesus prayed, "*Father...not My will, but Yours be done*" (Luke 22:42). In the latter part of his life of love for God, the Apostle John spoke of faith that overcomes the world (I John 5:4), and that you can actually know God (I John 5:20). John tells us, then, that faith grows until you can have victory over the world now. You can come to know God, increasingly. Faith is a gift that increasingly grows as we exercise it, much like our muscles grow when we exercise them.

It is time to get out of the boat!

Where does God intend for us to go in our faith? If we can name specific destinations, we end with the wrong focus, which is on ourselves. The primary goal of faith is to focus us on Jesus Christ. Furthermore, the Bible states that we are strengthened with power through God's Spirit, Jesus Christ's indwelling. It speaks of a place you can reach quickly, of you understanding the love of Christ that is actually beyond hu-

27: CALLED INTO A LIFE BY FAITH

man knowledge; a place where you are filled with God's fullness. (Read Ephesians 3:16-19). Never forget, as mentioned in chapter ten of this book, "Faith Moves Beyond the Ordinary."

That faith introduced you into the life that is now yours as an adopted son or daughter of God. That is exactly why Jesus said, *"Nothing will be impossible to you"* (**Matthew 17:20**). This truth puts you in a new, challenging and risky place since the presence of doubt cancels out our receiving anything from God (James 1:6-7). We are challenged to live in a place that is absent of all doubt, even those little shadows of doubt in us from which we often excuse as "little" doubts. There is no such thing as "little" doubt. There is belief and unbelief. As faith changes you, you will never be the same. You begin to experience startling miracles as faith sets you in the supernatural. As people saw the things God does through His children, others were struck with awe and amazement. Don't you know that those God used to express such kingdom truths also felt that awe and amazement? They were instruments that God could use because they looked beyond the natural to what God could do through them.

Do we understand how God has rescued us out of a world that sin has turned upside down. Faith is God's gift to us that turns the world back right side up. Remember, before we knew Jesus Christ, we were part of that world that believed right side up is upside down. Therefore, at times the expression of this new life seems strange, even beyond our comprehension. This new life is strange and beyond the understanding of the world and its ways. It takes us time to get beyond the normal, upside down way of living we left behind. We enter into the world

DOORWAYS to Greater Faith

that is turned right side up. It takes time to develop customary habits in faith for us to begin to fully enter into it.

Jesus tells us that He has victory over the world. So, too, do we who belong to God through our faith in Jesus Christ. It takes time for us to make that adjustment. Friend, it doesn't take much time. You can adjust right now. Faith in God, in God's existence and promises, allows us to obey God as he leads us into activities that redeem and reclaim those lives God wants for His own. Faith will continue to grow in us as we will continually see the wonders produced by it. In Jesus' Words, your prayers get answered and wonders occur through you, *"according to your faith;"* according to your relationship and intimacy with God. See Matthew 9:29. The more real your faith, the less real your doubts. You are freed from doubt and reign over the world where you live.

Faith steps out of the human situation and into the hands of God. Peter stepped out of the boat and walked on water, when Jesus told him to come. As long as his heart was on Jesus no doubt entered, and he walked on water, like Jesus. As God worked through an imperfect man such as Peter, He will work through you. It is time to get out of the boat!

Later, Peter raised Tabitha from the dead (Acts 9:40). Notice that Peter did not go into lengthy prayer over Tabitha. He knelt and sought God's will. Peter heard God's answer, turned, and without even standing up, he didn't pray any more. He commanded: *"Tabitha, arise."* He did not attract attention to himself. He let the people see what God does through the gift of faith He has given. Jesus did all of His works as God com-

27: CALLED INTO A LIFE BY FAITH

manded Him in order to reveal what *you* can do by faith; to reveal what *we* can do by faith. Peter is God's example of what you can do by faith, faith that is focused on God and His will. Peter wasn't alone. God used His servants John, Paul, Stephen, all those mentioned in Hebrews 11 in which He mentioned numerous unnamed others, men and women of whom the world was not worthy. Many had no worldly possessions, and like Jesus, not even a place to lay their heads. Some of them lived in holes in the ground. They had one possession: Faith.

There is always more to say about faith and its wonders as it opens one's life to a present and supernatural state. One final truth for us is found here: *"For if by the transgression of one, death reigned through the one (Adam), much more those who received the abundance of grace and of the gift of righteousness will reign in life through the One, Jesus Christ"* (Romans 5:17).

As we reign over our words, what we say, we can reign over our thoughts, over our temper, our disposition, habits, morality, and over our passions, responses, and fears; and over everything else that is in our hearts. Through the gift of faith, Jesus gives you authority, a power that belongs to the surrendered believer to live a life beyond the ordinary — the life and walk of faith that God has prepared for you. It is time to walk through the doorways to greater faith.

LaVergne, TN USA
29 January 2010
171519LV00008B/16/P